For the Love of

LABRADOR RETRIEVERS

For the Love of
LABRADOR RETRIEVERS

Robert Hutchinson

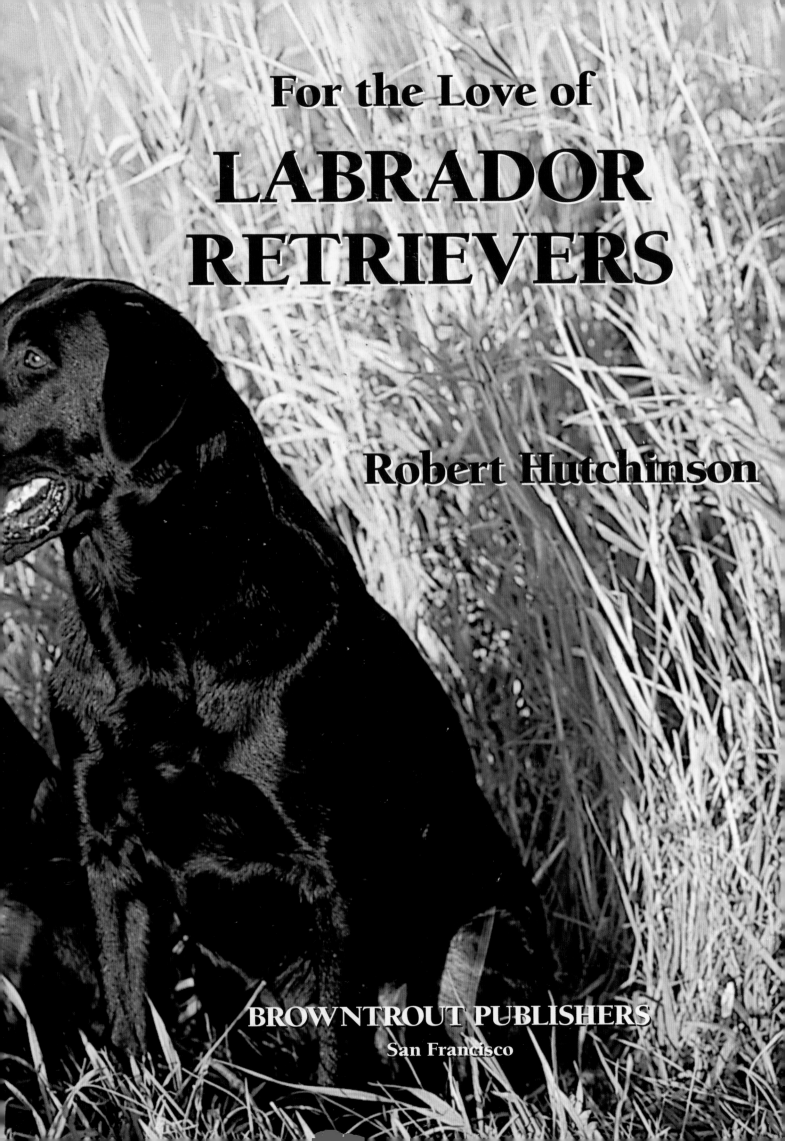

BROWNTROUT PUBLISHERS

San Francisco

Labrador Retrievers Photography Credits

Front Cover		©1998 Mark Raycroft
Back Cover		©1998 Denver Bryan
p.2/3		©1998 Mark Raycroft
5		©1998 Zandria Muench Beraldo
6		©1998 Denver Bryan
7		©1998 Denver Bryan
8		©1998 Sharon Eide & Elizabeth Flynn
10		©1998 Dwight Dyke
11	(top)	©1998 Zandria Muench Beraldo
11	(bottom)	©1998 Denver Bryan
12		©1998 Mark Raycroft
14		©1998 Jerry Shulman
16/17		©1998 Mark Raycroft
18		©1998 Mark Raycroft
20		©1998 Mark Raycroft
22		©1998 Howard Weamer
23	(top)	©1998 Howard Weamer
23	(bottom)	©1998 Mark Raycroft
24		©1998 Mark Raycroft
26		©1998 Mark Raycroft
27	(top)	©1998 Mark Raycroft
27	(bottom)	©1998 Zandria Muench Beraldo
28		©1998 Kent & Donna Dannen
30/31		©1998 Dwight L. Dyke
32		©1998 Kent & Donna Dannen
36		©1998 Zandria Muench Beraldo
34/35		©1998 Sharon Eide & Elizabeth Flynn
38		©1998 Denver Bryan
39	(top)	©1998 Mark Raycroft
39	(bottom)	©1998 Sharon Eide & Elizabeth Flynn
40		©1998 Denver Bryan
41	(top)	©1998 Howard Weamer
41	(bottom)	©1998 Zandria Muench Beraldo
42/43		©1998 Denver Bryan
44		©1998 Zandria Muench Beraldo
46/47		©1998 Londie G. Padelsky
48		©1998 Mark Raycroft
49	(top)	©1998 Mark Raycroft
49	(bottom)	©1998 Sharon Eide & Elizabeth Flynn
50		©1998 Howard Weamer
52		©1998 Mark Raycroft
53	(top)	©1998 Mark Raycroft
53	(bottom)	©1998 Howard Weamer
54		©1998 Mark Raycroft
56/57		©1998 Denver Bryan
58		©1998 Mark Raycroft
60		©1998 Jerry Shulman
62/63		©1998 Denver Bryan
64		©1998 Mark Raycroft
66		©1998 Mark Raycroft
67	(top)	©1998 Kent & Donna Dannen
68		©1998 Zandria Muench Beraldo
69	(top)	©1998 Kent & Donna Dannen
69	(bottom)	©1998 Kent & Donna Dannen
70		©1998 Howard Weamer
72/73		©1998 Zandria Muench Beraldo
74		©1998 Mark Raycroft
76		©1998 Howard Weamer
78		©1998 Mark Raycroft
80/81		©1998 Mark Raycroft
82		©1998 Mark Raycroft
83		©1998 Mark Raycroft
84		©1998 Kent & Donna Dannen
86/87		©1998 Mark Raycroft
88		©1998 Mark Raycroft
90		©1998 Denver Bryan
91	(top)	©1998 Sharon Eide & Elizabeth Flynn
91	(bottom)	©1998 Jerry Shulman
92		©1998 Mark Raycroft
94/95		©1998 Howard Weamer
96		©1998 Howard Weamer
98		©1998 Dwight L. Dyke
100		©1998 Mark Raycroft
101	(top)	©1998 Mark Raycroft
102/103		©1998 Mark Raycroft
104		©1998 Mark Raycroft
106		©1998 Denver Bryan
108/109		©1998 Zandria Muench Beraldo
110		©1998 Mark Raycroft
112		©1998 Howard Weamer

Library of Congress Cataloging-in-Publication Data
Hutchinson, Robert, 1951 —
    Labrador retrievers / Robert Hutchinson.
        p.   cm. — (For the love of—)
        ISBN 1-56313-904-9 (alk. paper)
        1. Labrador retriever. 2. Labrador retriever — Pictorial works.
    I. Title.   II. Series: Hutchinson, Robert, 1951–   For the love of—
    SF429.L3H88   1998
    636.752'7 — dc21

                                                            98-39142
                                                               CIP

Printed and bound in Italy by Milanostampa

ISBN: 1-56313-904-9 (alk. paper)
10 9 8 7 6 5 4 3 2 1
Digit on the right indicates the number of this printing

Published by:
BrownTrout Publishers, Inc.
Post Office Box 280070
San Francisco, California 94128-0070 U.S.A.

Toll Free: 800 777 7812
Website: browntrout.com

The author gratefully acknowledges the
archival assistance of Glenda Dawe, Centre for Newfoundland Studies,
Memorial University of Newfoundland, St. John's.

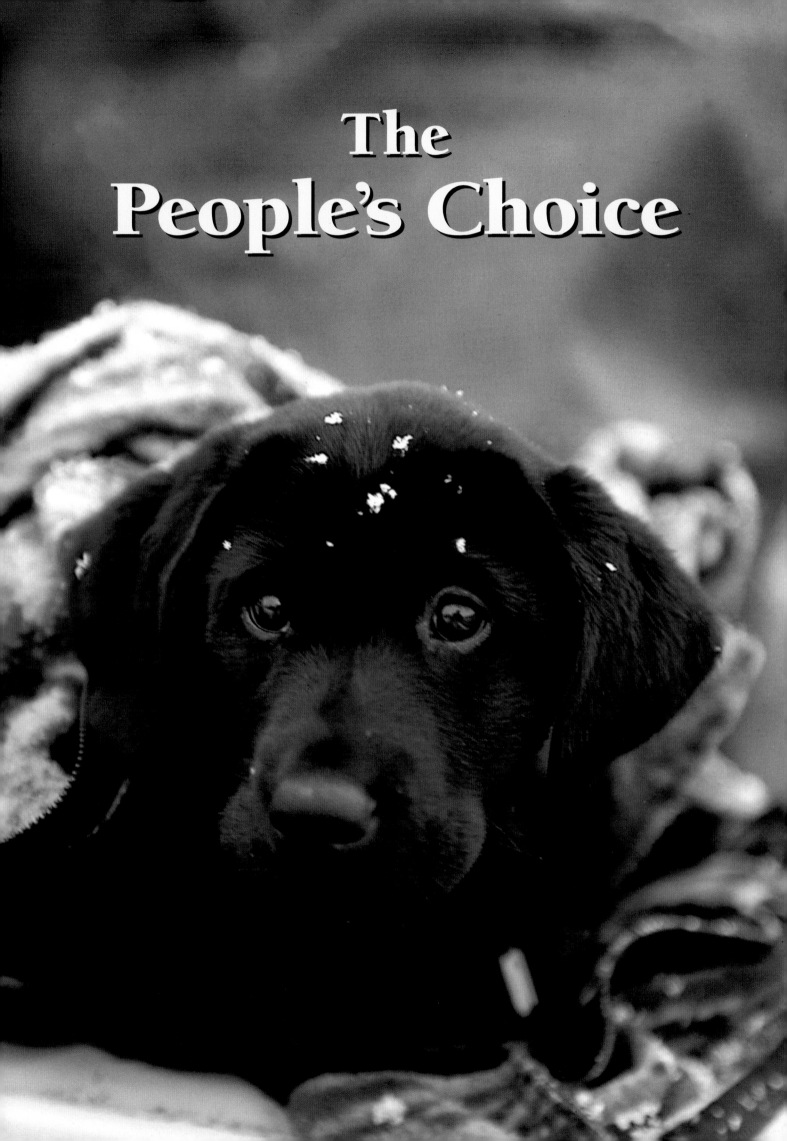

The People's Choice

Suppose for a moment that you were the leader of the most powerful nation in the world; that you suffered unlimited exposure to the public eye but also enjoyed unlimited means of canvassing public opinion; and, finally, that you were desirous of an attractive, intelligent, and stable confidant whose character was unimpeachable and who could never be subpoenaed. Who would you choose to be your high-profile buddy? If recent events are any indication, you would choose a Lab.

And odds are, you would make the same choice even if you were just an ordinary American citizen. For the Labrador Retriever is far and away the most popular dog breed in the United States today. It has been pulling away from the competition since it climbed into first place in AKC registrations in 1991. Based on its 158,366 registrations in 1997, the Lab is currently more than twice as popular as any runner-up breed. The Lab is also the most popular breed in its FCI country of origin — Britain — with over 32,000 KC registrations.

Although the breed has of late been surging to registration numbers unprecedented in the history of the dog fancy, the ascendancy of the Lab is no ephemeral quirk of fashion. The breed's popularity is a natural outcome of the growing public recognition of its singular mix of solid qualities. Its winning combination of physical versatility, mental resourcefulness, and emotional equanimity enables the Lab to adapt superbly to any of a diverse range of work and play environments. From the most specialized to the most generalized, very few canine jobs fall outside the competence of the Lab. Whether it be retrieving game for the hunter, guiding the blind, consoling the shut-in, or frolicking with the children, the Lab tackles every assigned task with seriousness, steadiness, affability, and — most characteristically — with quiet joy in the exercise of its ample talents and judgment.

One task, however, stands foremost as proper to — and dearest to the heart of — the Labrador Retriever. It is, of course, retrieving. Five other Retrievers are also bred in the United States today: the Golden Retriever, the Chesapeake Bay Retriever, the Flat-Coated Retriever, the Curly-Coated Retriever, and the Nova Scotia Duck Tolling Retriever. Yet, in open-breed field trials, the Lab consistently proves itself the cock of the walk at retrieving. As a matter of fact, every National Field Trial Champion (winner of the annual National Retriever Championship Open Stake) since 1952 has been a Lab!

Not that any of these competing Retriever breeds could by any stretch be considered a slouch. For they are all scions of the same stock as the Lab. The genotypes of the six modern Retriever breeds are all more or less closely related to one another insofar as they share a certain nineteenth-century common ancestor: an extinct maritime working-dog type known (along with many other names) as *the St. John's breed of the Newfoundland Dog*. The distinctions amongst the modern Retrievers in respect of this hardy precursor are but a matter of degree. The Lab is simply that common ancestor's most direct descendant going into the twenty-first century.

The Lab's glamorous cousin, the Golden Retriever, has also been shooting to stardom. It now ranks as the fourth most popular breed in the United States. Its 70,158 AKC registrations in 1997 put the Golden Retriever just behind the German Shepherd and Rottweiler and gaining rapidly. Just what is it about Retrievers — and the Labrador Retriever is unquestionably the Retriever *par excellence* — that makes them such deuced good all-round dogs?

The Lab is good at just about everything because it was developed to be so amazingly good at one thing in particular. The retrieving function to which the Retriever was bred makes multifarious mental demands upon the dog. To be capable of acquiring and applying the complex functional skills necessary in retrieving, the Retriever must evince, on one hand, extraordinary tractability and educability with respect to its master's cues; on the other hand, strong initiative and drive outside the purview of its master's control while on a blind retrieve. It is this balanced assemblage of complementary qualities, originally instilled in the Retriever for just one specialized function, that gives the Retriever the responsive flexibility to be good at just about anything.

No less stringent than the mental demands are the physical demands made upon the Retriever in the execution of its retrieving function. And in no Retriever breed is the marriage of form and function more harmoniously realized than in the Labrador Retriever. The form of the Labrador Retriever follows its function as a gun dog designed to retrieve game on land and in water.

To move efficiently over difficult terrain while lugging a fat pheasant or goose in its mouth, the Lab must be strong — yet not lumbering — in construction. Moreover, to last all day at such strenuous work, the Lab must husband its strength by economy of movement. Its gait must be long, level, and smooth. Stamina, no less than strength, is required in the Labrador Retriever's job. But the body form that optimizes strength in weight-lifting is quite different from the body form that optimizes stamina in running and swimming. The Lab's form — made up of hard-muscled curves that flow powerfully into one another without jinking over any sharp angles — represents the most ergonomic solution to the multiple physical functions required of the Lab.

According to the Standards of both the British and American Labrador Retriever Clubs, four features are specially diagnostic of the breed. These are its head, tail, coat, and temperament. The form of each of these features serves in its own precise way the Lab's overall retrieving function.

With respect to the Lab's head, the skull is impressively broad and fronted by a moderate stop. The muzzle is broad, deep, and strong — as it must be to keep its grip on a deadweight of game while the rest of the dog abandons itself to swimming, running, leaping ditches, and crashing through thickets. The length of the Lab's straight muzzle from its dark nose to its stop almost equals the length of its rounded skull from stop to occiput. Set well apart on either side of the stop are those dark "burnt sugar" eyes that so eloquently bespeak the Lab's bonhomie and intelligence. On level with the eyes and well behind on the head are set the Lab's rather short, close, pendant ears.

The second diagnostic feature of the Labrador Retriever is its tail. The Lab's densely coated "otter" tail is muscular, thick-based, and tapered for better ruddering in water. On land, the Lab ordinarily carries its tail on a level that extends the slightly sloping line of the croup. The tail's action is one of measured pleasure rather than flighty gaiety.

The third diagnostic feature of the Labrador Retriever is its coat. Ever ready to dive into cold water after fallen fowl, the Lab is clad in a double-ply wet suit that is oiled to shed water. A soft, dense undercoat provides impermeability and insulation. A short, hard outer coat armors the Lab against the pricks and scrapes of swampwater and underbrush.

The correct Lab coat comes in one of three basic colors: *black, yellow,* or *chocolate.* Whereas *black* Labs are all uniformly black, *yellow* Labs range the spectrum from off-white through golden yellow to fox-red. Moreover, a *yellow* Lab's ears, back, and underparts are commonly a different shade of *yellow* than the rest of its body. *Chocolate* Labs range over many hues of purply brown — from wilted lilac through boiled liver to bittersweet mousse.

Which one of the three basic coat colors a given Lab ends up wearing is completely determined by just two pairs of genes that combine by straightforward Mendelian rules. These simple rules constrain the possible colors of the progeny of two Labs of the same color: Two *black* parents can sometimes beget all three colors in the same litter; Two *yellow* parents must always throw all-yellow litters; Two *chocolate* parents will never have a black puppy. Because the coat-color genes interact independently of all other genes, old notions that the three groups of Labs as defined by coat color also differ systematically in other characteristics must be put down to stiff-necked delusion.

The fourth — and, as we have seen, the most critical — diagnostic feature of the Labrador Retriever is its temperament. Seminal to the foundation stock of every one of our six modern Retriever breeds, as we have noted, is the St. John's breed of the Newfoundland Dog. Moreover, in the closing decades of the nineteenth century, prior to the stabilization of our modern stud-lines under the aegis of dedicated breed clubs, extensive cross-breeding amongst the nascent Retriever breeds was practiced by experimentalists seeking the formula for the ideal gun dog. Given the multiplex congruences and interminglings in their breeding histories, it is not surprising that the Retriever breeds all show broad similarities in temperament and behavior.

The Lab shares with all other Retrievers the following traits: inexhaustible retrieving drive; joy in the sights and sounds of the hunt; delight in diving and swimming; slow mental maturation; stable and cheerful disposition; unconditional love toward master; affability toward strangers; hardness against pain; negligible attack instinct; and "sagacity" (intelligence employing complex branch-routines that mimic reason). This last trait stands out as the signature contribution of the St. John's breed of the Newfoundland Dog and is more strongly preserved in the Labrador than any other Retriever breed.

Retrievers were stamped with their fixed and enduring form in the nineteenth century by breeders of the British hunting aristocracy whose sole aim was to optimize their dogs' functionality as retrievers of the dead or wounded birds that they had shot out of the air over land or water. Nowadays, by contrast, many Retriever dogs are bred for show or companionship rather than the field. As a result, each Retriever breed has bifurcated into two increasingly distinct sub-breeds: the tough-as-nails field dog, still judged for performance alone; and the gorgeous show dog, judged for beauty of form (as codified in the relevant breed standard) divorced from function. The show Retriever tends to be larger and more phlegmatic than its field counterpart.

A strong index of this bifurcating tendency in the Retriever breeds has been the wane of dual champions. In the early decades of a breed's national development, it was standard for outstanding individual Retrievers to win both field and bench championships. In later decades, such dual achievement has become almost unheard of. Within the Labrador Retriever breed in Britain, for example, nine Dual Champions emerged beginning in 1922; after 1949, not one. Allowing for the later introduction of the breed to the United States, a similar trend is evident here: in the half-century following 1941, thirty-five American Labs earned the title of Dual Champion; in the quarter-century since 1983, not one.

Even so, those modern Retriever dogs that have been neither bred nor trained to the field do retain their ancestral retrieving aptitudes in large — albeit diminishing — measure. Different fortes in this shared repertoire distinguish one Retriever breed from another. The Golden excels in bench and obedience trials. The Chessie performs outstandingly over open water. And the Lab? Thanks to its matchless versatility and well-roundedness, the Lab garners a goodly share of wins in every realm of competition: show; obedience; tracking; guide work. The great forte of the Lab, however, reflects the predominance of the St. John's breed of the Newfoundland Dog in its ancestry. Thanks to its St. John's "sagacity," the Lab reigns today the undisputed sovereign of the whole realm of field trials.

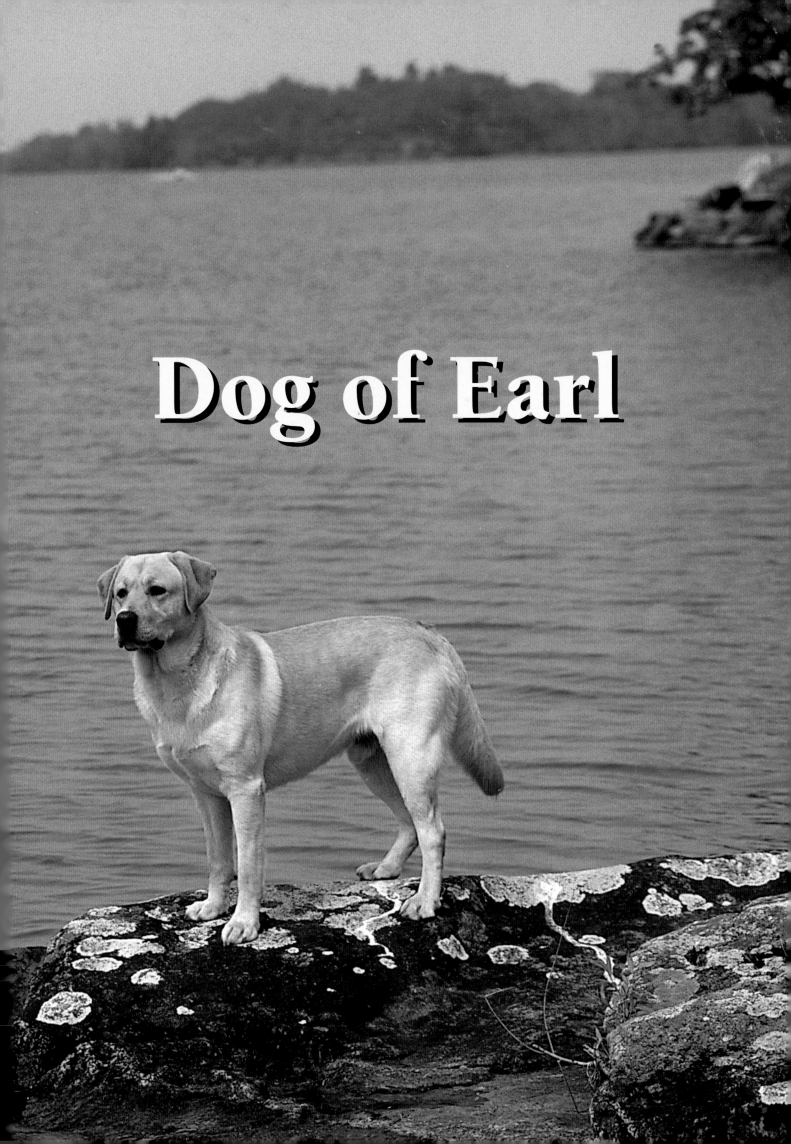

Dog of Earl

Although it now polls as the American people's dog of democratic choice, our modern Labrador Retriever traces its pedigree straight back to the tightly intertwined breed lines of the private kennels of two suffocatingly patrician and opulently privileged hunting sets in nineteenth-century Britain. The principal figures of these two sets — the Dukes of Buccleuch and the Earls of Home in the northern set; the Earls of Malmesbury in the southern set — all breathed the rarefied Tory atmosphere at the apex of the British landed aristocracy.

The critical conjunction in the development and launching of the Labrador Retriever breed came about in the early 1880s when two members of the northern set (the 6th Duke of Buccleuch and the 12th Earl of Home) went on beach holiday together and bumped into a local member of the southern set (the 3rd Earl of Malmesbury). The (actually soon-to-be) 6th Duke of Buccleuch (William Henry Walter Montagu Douglas Scott; 1831-1914; would soon succeed to his dukedom, 1884; styled for the nonce "Lord Dalkeith") and the 12th Earl of Home (1834-1918; having just succeeded to earldom, 1881) came down together several times from their neighboring estates in the fabled "Scott Country" of the Scottish Borders to winter in Bournemouth on the southern coast of England. This Dorset seaside resort on Poole Bay enjoyed such a reputation for palmy elegance in the nineteenth century that Thomas Hardy described it (under the name of "Sandbourne") in *Tess of the D'Urbervilles* (1891) as the "Mediterranean lounging-place on the English Channel."

Neither the ducal heir apparent nor his good buddy the earl was your run-of the-mill forty-something titled beach bum. Each sat on family holdings of almost regal grandeur and venerability. Each was born a Border clan chief to boot.

The 6th Duke of Buccleuch's eponymous ancestor, the 1st Duke, was Monmouth — the well-favored but ill-starred bastard of Charles II. The 6th Duke's father, the 5th Duke of Buccleuch, had been Keeper of the Privy Seal (1842-46) and Lord President of the Council (1846) in Sir Robert Peel's Conservative government. At the time of his Bournemouth holidays, Lord Dalkeith himself (the 6th Duke-to-be) had just wound up a long career in the House of Commons as Conservative MP for Midlothian (1853-1868 and 1874-1880). His wife, the daughter of the 1st Duke of Abercorn, was Mistress of the Robes to Queen Victoria. Upon his succession a couple of years hence, the 6th Duke of

Buccleuch would come into the second vastest estate in Britain (720 square miles) and find himself — measured by his annual income of £217,163 — the wealthiest individual in Britain. Today, the 400 square-mile estate of the 9th Duke of Buccleuch has advanced in rank to the largest in Britain. The Dukes of Buccleuch are the hereditary chiefs of Clan Scott.

Lord Dalkeith's sidekick was no lightweight either. The 12th Earl of Home's eponymous ancestor, the 1st Earl of Home (1566-1619), had accompanied James VI to London in 1603 and positioned himself as one of James I's best-rewarded favorites. The 12th Earl's descendant, the 14th Earl, who died in 1995, put in a turn as the Prime Minister of Great Britain (1963-64) — in tandem with his hereditary job as Chief of Clan Home. Only twenty miles of undulating upland separate the Duke of Buccleuch's main residence of Bowhill — graced to this day by paintings of Leonardo da Vinci and Gainsborough — from the Earl of Home's stately Hirsel.

Now it came to pass that the elderly 3rd Earl of Malmesbury (1807-1889) invited the 6th Duke of Buccleuch and the 12th Earl of Home for a spot of shooting at Heron Court (alternately spelled *Hurn Court*) — his neogothic manor set in a rhododendron forest just a few miles north of Bournemouth on the Hampshire side of the River Avon. As a Conservative politician, the 3rd Earl of Malmesbury commanded his guests' unqualified respect . Like the 6th Duke of Buccleuch's father, he had twice been Keeper of the Privy Seal (1866-68, in the government of the Earl of Derby; and 1874-76, in the government of Benjamin Disraeli); in addition, he had twice been Secretary of State for Foreign Affairs (1852 and 1858-59, in two earlier governments of the Earl of Derby).

Yet, from the vantage of the British class order, the 3rd Earl of Malmesbury's title could not begin to rival in dignity or antiquity those of his younger guests. Son of a brilliant but untitled grammarian, the 1st Earl of Malmesbury (1746-1820) had earned his own ennoblement as a reward for his many signal services to the Crown as a career diplomatist. This hardworking civil servant was not created Earl of Malmesbury until the end of his service in 1800.

No less wide than the social distance between the 3rd Earl of Malmesbury and his Scottish guests yawned the discrepancy in their landed wealth. Although the grounds of Heron Court were extensive by southern standards, they were really

insignificant compared to the northern duchies of his guests. Nevertheless, Heron Court did contain two sporting treasures which even these two visiting super-grandees must envy of the old Earl of Malmesbury: an extraordinary abundance of wildfowl and an extraordinary breed of water dog to retrieve them.

The grounds of Heron Court then encompassed a swathe of the flood plain shared by the Rivers Strout, Moors, and Avon. This little flood plain straddles the Dorset-Hampshire border and is abutted on the east by the 93,000-acre New Forest, preserved in semi-natural state since William the Conqueror. Most of the grounds of Heron Court were altered beyond recognition when they were commandeered for D-Day support operations during the Second World War. The marshy flatland was drained and covered by the runways of what is now the Bournemouth International Airport.

Back in the 1880s, however, the undrained marshes supported a very different kind of fly-way. From late September through February, the Heron Court marshes abounded in waterfowl that flocked south to winter in the estuaries or — when the winter was hard — to muster strength to cross the Channel. In consequence, Heron Court seasonally offered first-class "shore-shooting": the eminently Victorian sport of blasting away constant-fire at dense gaggles of wildfowl that briefly clutter the sky over coastal marshes either at dawn as they head offshore or at dusk as they return.

To retrieve the great numbers of birds shot down in his palustral aviary, the 3rd Earl of Malmesbury kept his Heron Court kennel well stocked with an extraordinary water-retriever breed that was his own especial creature and abiding study. As he was to write to the 6th Duke of Buccleuch a few years later in 1887: "We always call mine Labrador dogs and I have kept the breed as pure as I could from the first I had from Poole, at that time carrying on a brisk trade with Newfoundland. The real breed may be known by their having a close coat which turns the water off like oil and, above all, a tail like an otter."

The 3rd Earl of Malmesbury derived his Heron Court strain of "Labrador dogs" from retriever-type dogs imported from Newfoundland by cod fishermen out of Poole, just eight miles down the road from Heron Court. In point of fact, both the 6th Duke of Buccleuch and the 12th Earl of Home had since their youth been intimately familiar with this type of dog imported from Newfoundland. For both their fathers — the 5th Duke of Buccleuch (1806-1884) and the 11th Earl of Home (1799-1881) — had in their hunting heyday (1830s through 1860s) kept their kennels stocked with retrieving dogs imported from Newfoundland through the Scottish codfleet port of Greenock. In the

1870s, however, these two aging lords had permitted their lines of Newfoundland dogs to peter out. By the early 1880s, the only Newfoundland retrievers left in Britain were to be found in three estate kennels of the southern set (the 3rd Earl of Malmesbury's Heron Court; Mr C.J. Radclyffe's Hyde; and Lord Wimborne's Canford — all stocked by importations through Poole) and in three estate kennels of the northern set (Sir Frederick Graham's Netherby; the 12th Duke of Hamilton's Hamilton Palace; and the 8th Lord Ruthven's Winton — all derived from the importations of the 5th Duke of Buccleuch and 10th Earl of Home through Greenock).

Several probable causes might be adduced for the desuetude of the Buccleuch and Home lines of Newfoundland retrievers in the 1870s.

On the personal front, the fathers themselves were grown too old to hunt; and their sons were preoccupied with their political careers in London. On the economic front, commerce all but ceased between Scotland and Newfoundland during the crash of the cod population in the Newfoundland fisheries that persisted from 1860 to 1868. As a result, the Scottish kennels were starved of three generations of replacement stock from Newfoundland. The Newfoundland fisheries did finally recover in 1869, but just six years later the onset of ruinous weather in Britain conspired with the flooding of the British market by cheap American prairie grain to precipitate the Great Agricultural Depression that prostrated rural Britain beginning in 1875. The unprecedented business difficulties in which the Depression mired the vast estates of the Scottish lords diverted their attention from their wonted leisure pursuits.

Not being an agricultural landowner of any consequence, the 3rd Earl of Malmesbury suffered no such distraction from his cherished "Labrador dog" breeding program. Since his birth, the 3rd Earl of Malmesbury had been familiar with the imported Newfoundland retrieving dogs that figured in the Heron Court kennel during the tenures of both his father and grandfather.

The 1st Earl of Malmesbury — upon quitting his glittering international career on account of worsening deafness in 1797 — retired to the benefice of Heron Court in 1800, where he quietly dwelt as a sort of rustic Nestor until his death in 1820; whereupon his son, James Edward Harris (1778-1841), became the 2nd Earl of Malmesbury. Upon his arrival at Heron Court in 1801 at the age of 23, James took up fowling with all the zest and skill that his father had lavished on delicate diplomatic manoeuvres. James' passion for fowling never flagged thereafter, as is manifest in published extracts from his voluminous hunting journals which detail his daily outings through the years. His hunting journal for 1809 contains an entry which qualifies as the first extant British record of the use of a Newfoundland dog (which he bought in Poole from a codfleet captain who had shipped it from Newfoundland) as a gun dog. James' journals establish, therefore, that gun dogs imported from Newfoundland were kept in the Heron Court kennels during the tenure of his father, the 1st Earl of Malmesbury.

It is not known whether an unbroken Heron Court breed line of Newfoundland retrievers extended from the 1st Earl in the opening decade of the nineteenth century continuously to the 3rd Earl eight decades later. The Malmesbury breed line would have been vulnerable to interruption or deterioration whenever the current Earl would remove to London to serve a political appointment, such that the breed line might afterward have required restarting or recalibration with fresh imports. Soon after the title passed to him in 1820, for example, the 2nd Earl of Malmesbury was appointed Undersecretary for Foreign Affairs in Canning's ministry of 1822-27.

The 3rd Earl of Malmesbury's appointments to various senior ministries (1852, 1858-59, 1866-68, and 1874-76) had been, by contrast, more numerous but each of duration shorter than a single dog generation. We know from the above excerpt from the 3rd Earl of Malmesbury's letter of 1887 that he at least had succeeded in maintaining his own breed line of Newfoundland gundogs uninterruptedly: "We always call mine Labrador dogs and I have kept the breed as pure as I could from the first I had from Poole."

Note in this key sentence penned by the 3rd Earl of Malmesbury two ways that he did *not* write it. First, he did not write simply that he had "kept the breed pure" — but rather that he had "kept it as pure as I could." His form of expression seems careful to leave wriggle-room for the possibility that a little cross-breeding had taken place. This would hardly have been shocking or shameful, given that the received wisdom in Victorian sporting circles was that the best retrievers were spaniel-setter-Labrador crosses.

The second way that the 3rd Earl did not write the sentence was: "We have always called ours Labrador dogs and I have kept the breed as pure as I could from the first my father (or grandfather) had from Poole." His exclusive use of the first person singular supports the inference that the 3rd Earl of Malmesbury had had at some point in the past to restart the Malmesbury line of Newfoundland gundogs with fresh imports from Poole. But we also know that the 3rd Earl of Malmesbury had succeeded in breeding from his Poole imports a consistent strain of remarkably efficient gundogs.

So efficiently and indefatigably did the 3rd Earl of Malmesbury's strain of "Labrador dogs" perform as all-terrain retrievers that they excited the unrestrained admiration of his two high-born shooting guests from Scotland. As Lord George Scott — brother to the 7th Duke of Buccleuch, who died in 1935 — wrote in his contribution to Sprake's *The Labrador*

Retriever (1933): "Lord Dalkeith, afterwards the 6th Duke of Buccleuch, and the 12th Earl of Home both spent several winters at Bournemouth in the early eighties, and when shooting at Heron Court (where wild-duck shooting was first class), were amazed at the work of Lord Malmesbury's dogs, especially in water." This amazement of the Scots was doubtless heightened by eager considerations of the timeliness of the breed. For the decade in question was technologically ripe for a keen appreciation of the potential applications of Malmesbury's super-retrievers.

At that time, the standard fowling gun was a double 8-bore breech-loading shotgun with 30-in. barrels and weighing 15 lbs. In the two decades leading up to 1880, the breech-loading shotgun had been subjected to an accelerating cascade of technical improvements. In 1861, Daw had introduced into England the center-fire shotgun and cartridge, whose expansive case sealed off all escape of gas from the breech after detonation. In 1871, Murcott patented the first successful hammerless shotgun, in which the mechanism for

igniting the center-fire cartridges was contained entirely within the gun. In 1874, Needham introduced an automatic ejector mechanism for throwing out empty cartridge-cases. In 1875, Anson and Deeley introduced a new fore-end attachment that used the weight of the barrels to help cock the locks. The cumulative effect of this series of incremental improvements was to increase dramatically the shotgun's fire-rate and killing circles.

In consequence of these improvements to the shotgun, the number of birds that could be shot per shooter per outing had increased exponentially. But if the shooters were to exploit fully the new capabilities of their breech-loading shotguns, all the ancillary operations of the estate shooting party had likewise to be improved. The gamekeepers had to farm more game; the game-beaters had to concentrate the game in the field more effectively; the gun-loaders had to load more quickly: all to provide grist for the shotgun's increased fire-rate and killing circles.

In proportion to the increased slaughtering efficiency of these human agents of the hunt, increased efficiency demands were being imposed upon their canine retrievers of birds killed or crippled. A bird not retrieved was a bird not bagged; a bird not bagged was a bird not counted; and — lip service to "pretty shooting" aside — kill count was the ultimate competitive criterion of this supremely serious sporting contest amongst the rich and powerful of Imperial Britain.

During the second half of the nineteenth century, the Flat-coat Retriever had firmly established itself as the retriever of choice on British estates. This breed was elegantly hunky in body, flowing in coat, stylish in carriage, polite in manner, and perfectly adequate in performance to the work-rates required by the early breech-loaders. Unfortunately for the Flatcoat, each successive improvement to the shotgun was catching it a bit more flatfooted. The Flatcoat's bulky body and ambling carriage were resisting adaptation to the increasing demands for stamina and celerity in the field. The moment was ripe for the apotheosis of a new breed. Enter the Earl of Malmesbury's super-retriever.

The two Scots were amazed. And so gratified was he, in turn, by their amazement that "Lord Malmesbury gave some of his breed to both." The 3rd Earl of Malmesbury — seizing the opportunity in the twilight of his own life to entrust to financially competent gundog connoisseurs, whose gamekeepers had extensive breeding experience with Newfoundland retriever dogs, the perpetuation of his retrieving breed which he had sedulously preserved, refreshed, and refined over many decades — made his young guests the gift of six of his precious creations. And good thing he did: for the Heron Court kennel died out soon after the 3rd Earl of Malmesbury's death in 1889.

According to the ducal manuscript captioned *Pedigree of His Grace the Duke of Buccleuch's Labrador Retrievers as of August 1894*, the 6th Duke of Buccleuch received four of the 3rd Earl of Malmesbury's dogs:

1) NED [1882: Malmesbury's SWEEP (1877, a "Newfoundland") ex Malmesbury's JUNO (1878, a "Labrador")];

2) AVON [1885: Malmesbury's TRAMP (a "smooth coated") ex Malmesbury's JUNO (1878, a "Labrador")];

3) DINAH [1885: Malmesbury's NELSON (a "Longcoated Newfoundland") ex Malmesbury's NELL (1880, a "Straight coated")];

4) NELL [1886: "Lord Wimborne's Dog" (1882) ex Malmesbury's JUNO (1882, a "Labrador")].

[It should be noted that only one of the six parents of these four original gift dogs is described in the 1894 *Pedigree* as a "Labrador," the other five parents are variously described as a "Newfoundland," a "smooth coated," a "Long coated Newfoundland," a "Straight coated," and "Lord Wimborne's Dog." These are only a fraction of the bewildering assortment of ill-defined and often mutually contradictory terms that Victorian sportsmen adapted or coined to describe the variety of dogs from Newfoundland. The vexed question of what dog types might actually have been the referents of the various nomenclatures that nineteenth-century sportsmen idiosyncratically applied to the varieties of Newfoundland dogs will be addressed synoptically in the next chapter.]

As for the 12th Earl of Home, he received two of the 3rd Earl of Malmesbury's dogs: SMUT (1885; later given to Lord Cairns) and JUNO (1885; later given to F.P. Barnett).

These six gifts from the 3rd Earl of Malmesbury together account for the dominant portion of the ancestry of every Labrador Retriever registered in the world today. Of the six, Malmesbury's NED and AVON (both out of Malmesbury's JUNO) can lay particular claim to being the foundation sires of today's entire breed.

At first blush, the tracing of the lines of descent from the initial gifts to Buccleuch and Home from the 3rd Earl of Malmesbury's "Labrador dog" blood line in the 1880s to the

first entries of "Labrador Retrievers" in the Kennel Club Stud-book in 1903 promises only a labyrinthine exercise in pedantry. The long roster of grandiloquent names of the many breeders involved is daunting. Closer inspection reveals, however, that the lines of descent were neatly confined to the kennels of the two aforementioned geographic sets of noble sportsmen.

The northern set — centered upon the 6th Duke of Buccleuch and the 12th Earl of Home in the Scottish Lowlands — was ultra-aristocratic and included: Sir Frederick Graham of Netherby (who succeeded in 1861 to the baronetcy of his father, who had been Home Secretary and First Lord of the Admiralty); the Earl of Verulam (*aka* Viscount Grimston of the Irish peerage; son-in-law to Sir Frederick Graham of Netherby); the 12th Duke of Hamilton (1845-95; succeeded to the dukedom in 1863; the thirty-first richest individual in Great Britain in 1883; cousin to the 6th Duke of Buccleuch's wife); the 8th Lord Ruthven; Lord Alexander Fraser Saltoun (the eccentric violin-playing general of the Third China War of 1860); and the Honourable Arthur Holland-Hibbert (who eventually succeeded as the 3rd Viscount Knutsford only a few years before his death in 1935).

The southern set — centered upon the 3rd Earl of Malmesbury in the immediate environs of Bournemouth — was decidedly tackier and included: Lord Wimborne (*né* Ivor Guest; moneyed scion of the Guest dynasty of South Wales ironworks industrialists; created a baron by Disraeli only in 1880; an insufferable snob and social climber, much lampooned in *Truth* and *Vanity Fair* as "the paying Guest;" election-rigging autocrat of an historic village a few miles north of Bournemouth called Canford Magna, which his father bought up in 1848); the Honourable Montagu Guest (Ivor's son); and Mr. C.E. Radclyffe (of Hyde, Wareham — a town just across the harbor from Poole; father of Major C.J. Radclyffe). Lord George Scott wrote in 1933 that "between 1865 and 1875 [these four members of the southern set] bought a lot of black water dogs imported from Newfoundland by one Hawker, the owner of a trading schooner, which plied between Newfoundland and Poole."

Despite their social disparities, the core members of both sets arrived at an informal compact in 1888 (a year before the 3rd Earl of Malmesbury's death) to cooperate in a program to fix and propagate the outstanding performance qualities of the Malmesbury line. By the accord, Lord George Scott (the younger son of the 6th Duke of Buccleuch) was given charge of planning all matings amongst the Labrador dogs of the various estates of the 6th Duke of Buccleuch, the 12th Earl of Home, the 12th Duke of Hamilton, the 3rd Earl of Malmesbury, Lord Wimborne, and the Honourable Montagu Guest. In all, sixty gamekeepers came thereby under the direction of Lord George Scott, who entrusted them with at least one approved breeding specimen each.

"Labradors" bred by these core kennels were also made available for breeding purposes to certain peripheral members of the northern set who still had Newfoundland retrievers that were descended either from the defunct lines of the 5th Duke of Buccleuch and the 11th Earl of Home or else from the last wave of Newfoundland imports in the early 1870s. Significantly, the route to the modern institutionalized Labrador Retriever breed threads through one of these peripheral lines rather than proceeding by straight linebreeding from the core Malmesbury-derived lines. As a result, a considerable proportion of our modern Labrador Retriever's genetic patrimony derives from a miscellany of Newfoundland dogs extraneous to Malmesbury's line.

The seminal peripheral line that leads to the first entries of "Labrador Retrievers" in the Kennel Club Studbook in 1903 was initiated by a Scottish gamekeeper. In 1858, the 11th Earl of Home obliged his patrician friend Sir Frederick Graham of Netherby (whose annual estates income of £27,000 proved insufficient to reduce his inherited debt of £275,000) by releasing one of his gamekeepers, J. Craw, from his employment at Hirsel in order to manage Graham's kennels at Netherby (an estate which, though in Cumberland, is just 8 miles south of the Buccleuch estate of Langholm in Dumfries to which Malmesbury's NED was brought in 1883). Craw brought with him some of the 11th Earl of Home's and 5th Duke of Buccleuch's Newfoundlander stock with which to establish a Netherby line, the most influential sire of which proved to be *Netherby* KIELDER [1872: *Netherby* BOATSWAIN (imported from Newfoundland by 11th Earl of Home *c.*1870) ex *Netherby* NELL (from the 5th Duke of Buccleuch)].

About 1878, Sir Frederick Graham gave KIELDER to his son-in-law, the Earl of Verulam, to start his own line of Labradors. In 1884 , the Honourable A. Holland-Hibbert

acquired SYBIL (whelped 1884; inbred granddaughter of *Netherby* KIELDER) from the Earl of Verulam. Out of this bitch, who had none of the Malmesbury strain, Holland-Hibbert started his own *Munden* kennel. In 1897, Holland-Hibbert mated SYBIL's granddaughter *Munden* SARAH (wh. 1893) to *Buccleuch* NITH [1891: *Buccleuch* AVON (from Malmesbury) ex *Buccleuch* GIP, daughter of *Buccleuch* NELL (from Malmesbury)] to get *Munden* Sixty. In 1900, *Munden* Sixty sired [1897: ex *Munden* SCOTTIE, granddaughter of *Buccleuch* AVON] the celebrated "3 S's" litter — *Munden* SINGLE, *Sherfield* SPRATT, and *Munden* SENTRY — which proved to be the foundation of the Labrador Retriever breed.

In 1904, two of these three great-grandchildren twice-over of Malmesbury's AVON — *Munden* SINGLE and *Munden* SENTRY — joined *Munden* SOVEREIGN (*Munden* SINGLE's son, sired in 1902 by A. Nicholl's BRAYTON SIR RICHARD) in becoming the first "Labrador Retrievers" to be entered as a separate breed in the Kennel Club Studbook. It was not perhaps pure coincidence that *Munden*'s owner had been politically instrumental in persuading the Kennel Club to recognize the "Labrador Retriever" as a distinct breed acceptable for Studbook registration.

In short order, Holland-Hibbert's *Munden* prefix snapped up two more historic firsts: the first Labrador Retriever to win a place in field trial (*Munden* SINGLE, 1904) and the first one to win a bench championship (*Munden* BROOME PARK BOB, 1906). In light of his pioneering achievements for the breed, it is hardly surprising that the Hon. Holland-Hibbert took yet another first for himself. He presided as the first chairman of the Labrador Retriever Club (LRC) from its foundation in 1916 until his death in 1935.

Paradoxically, the LRC was formed in alarmed reaction to the successes the year before of a black "Labrador" named *Horton* MAX in winning two Challenge Certificates, including the Crufts CC. Nobody quarreled that MAX was not a splendidly handsome fellow. The problem was that his beauty was not that of a "Labrador". Max's sire was the purebred Flatcoated Retriever Ch. DARENTH. Stanley Duncan wrote in 1911, with "the beautiful flat-coat as a rival, the Labrador can scarcely ever hope to secure the premier position among our gundogs." Now the fear arose that, with the beautiful Flatcoat as an all-too-intimate ally, the Labrador could scarcely hope to survive as a separate breed.

What galled the Lab breeders who rallied behind Holland-Hibbert was that MAX's owner was perfectly within his rights in registering his cross-breed as a "Labrador". Until that time, the Kennel Club accepted mixed retrievers under whatever breed denomination the owner elected. Cross-breeds from Labs with Pointers, Fox Hounds, and any of the various other Retrievers were routinely being entered into competition as "Labradors" *tout court*. MAX's public successes as a "Labrador" galvanized the beleaguered Lab breeding community into taking formal action to counter the rampant adulteration of the old Newfoundland lines. The LRC was founded *in extremis* in order to mandate and enforce breed purity with Studbook and Standard.

In contrast to MAX's spurious claim, each of Holland-Hibbert's "3-S" siblings might lay an impeccable claim to being a genuine Labrador superstar or the progenitor of genuine Labrador superstars. *Munden* SINGLE was the first of the litter to bring glory to the breed, distinguishing herself as the first Labrador Retriever to place at a trial (Certificate of Merit at the International Gun-dog League's Trial, Sherbourne, 1904). Having placed four more times by 1907, *Munden* SINGLE was awarded the posthumous honor of being stuffed and donated to the British Museum as the type of her breed.

Her litter-mate, *Sherfield* SPRATT, was to make his historic mark, too — but two generations down the road. His grandson, Captain Archibald Butter's FTC PETER OF FASKELLY (wh. 1908), won immortality as both the first retriever to work in response to whistles and hand signals and the first Labrador Retriever to become a Field Trial champion (Retriever Champion Stake, 1911). PETER OF FASKELLY was very much a "3-S's" co-production, being simultaneously grandson to *Sherfield* SPRATT; grandson to *Munden* SOVEREIGN; great-grandson to *Munden* SINGLE; and great-grandson to *Munden* SENTRY! From PETER OF FASKELLY was descended Mrs. Quentin Dick's (later Lorna, Countess Howe; a founding officer in the Labrador Retriever Club, 1916) illustrious *Banchory* BOLO (wh. 1915) — the first British Dual Champion and the prepotent foundation of Countess Howe's highly influential dynasty of Banchory champions — including another three of the total of nine British Dual Champions (Dual Ch. *Banchory* SUNSPECK, wh. 1917; Dual Ch. *Bramshaw* BOB, wh. 1929; and Dual Ch. *Banchory* PAINTER, wh. 1930).

Banchory imports (*Banchory* TRUMP of Wingan; *Banchory* JETSAM; Field Ch *Banchory* VARNISH of Wingan; the litters of three bitches in whelp to Dual Ch. *Bramshaw* BOB; etc., etc.) formed the spearhead of the Lab invasion of the United States that began in earnest in 1931. These *Munden*-blood imports were selected for the fledgling American Lab kennels by Scottish gamekeepers (Dave Elliot for J.F. Carlisle's Wingan; Tom Briggs and Jim Cowie for W. Averell Harriman's Arden; Douglas Marshall for Marshall Field's Caumset; Colin Macfarlane for Robert Goulet's Blake) who had themselves been imported by a sporting set of American millionaire Anglophiles-wannabe-aristocrats. This exclusive set enjoyed meeting on Goulet's broad 8,000-acre Glenmere Court estate on Long Island to recreate Victorian farmed-game sport on a scale that the declining British aristocracy had largely been compelled to abandon.

Marshall Field III (heir to the $125,000,000 Chicago department-store fortune; founder of the *Chicago Sun*) went often to Scotland for estate-hunting and came back with not only a Scottish gamekeeper and Scottish dogs but also a Scottish

wife (Mrs. Audrey James Field, the former Mrs. Dudley Coates of Perthshire; a great fancier of Yellows; the first President of The Labrador Retriever Club, Inc., 1931-1935). W. Averell Harriman (heir to the robber baron of Union Pacific Railroad, to the chairmanship of which he succeeded; ambassador to Great Britain and the Soviet Union; Governor of New York; eminent statesman, diplomat, and philanthropist) established in 1931 America's most influential early Lab kennel, Arden — named for his vast Scottish-style estate in the Hudson Highlands of New York. In 1910, the eighteen-year-old Averell Harriman presented 10,000 acres carved from his 30,000-acre Arden estate as a gift to New York State to be the rump of its future Harriman and Bear Mountain State Parks.

The Arden breeding program culminated in the famous "fish" litter of 1939, which included Paul Bakewell III's celebrated Dual Ch. SHED of Arden, three-time National Field Trial Champion. Averell Harriman stopped entering his string of champions in competition in 1940 after his Scottish gamekeeper was killed and he was called to Washington by FDR to expedite the war effort. So much for the international repercussions of the second of Holland-Hibbert's famous "3-S's" siblings.

The third of the "3 S's" — *Munden* SENTRY — stamped his imprint on the breed not only via his great-grandson PETER OF FASKELLY but also

via another of his progeny. His great-granddaughter, Lord Feversham's NEWTON BROWNIE (wh. 1908), was a key ingredient in the development of the modern Yellow Labrador Retriever. She was folded into a line descended from the first Labrador of yellow color to be registered (Major C.E. Radclyffe's BEN HYDE, wh. 1899) by Major and Mrs. Arthur Wormald, who presided successively over the Yellow Labrador Retriever Club from its founding in 1924 until Mrs. Veronica Wormald's death in 1979. Descending from NEWTON BROWNIE were the superlative crop of Yellow Lab champions produced by the Wormald's Knaith kennel in Scotland. This line culminated in Dual Ch. *Knaith* BANJO (wh. 1946; dual title 1949; died 1961), the great Yellow who stands to this day as the last British Dual Champion Lab. (In view of the essential part played by the "northern set" in the organized development of the Labrador Retriever breed, it is not surprising that fully five of the nine British Dual Champions were Scottish-bred.)

Strikingly, the only other Yellow Lab ever to secure a British Dual Championship had done so just two years before, in 1947: Mr. Edgar Winter's Dual Ch. STAINDROP SAIGHDEAR (who, by way of Dual Ch. *Banchory* BOLO's line, was himself descended from the "3 S's"). We have noted how the incompatible selective pressures of field and bench competition promote over the passage of decades a bifurcation of an originally homomorphous working breed into two distinct sub-types. We have also noted that the national Lab breed-split took full effect some forty years later in the United States than in Britain because the American breed started up some forty years later (yet early enough that the founding British imports were still of the original unitary working-type).

The last two British Dual Champions happened both to be Yellow Labs by an analogous process. Yellow Labs bifurcated later than Black Labs because the Yellow Labrador Club did not emerge to advance the claim of Yellows to fully competitive status until 1924 — twenty years after Black Labs had became firmly established in competition. Similarly in the United States, the only three Yellow Labs to achieve Dual Championship all appeared among the most recent third of the thirty-five Dual Champions. Although the evolutionary clocks of the British Labs, American Labs, Black Labs, and Yellow Labs all started running at different points in time, each of these four breeding populations eventually reached the same point of bifurcation into sub-types.

The key inference to be drawn from our cursory review of the foundation pedigrees of the Labrador Retriever breed is that — although certain peripheral lines from non-Malmesbury ancestors (notably *Netherby* KIELDER 1872, the 8th Lord Ruthven's JET, the 12th Duke of Hamilton's SAM 1884, and Major Radclyffe's BEN HYDE 1899) have undeniably been important to the breed's development — the lion's share of the genetic credit for the modern Lab must fall to the 3rd Earl of Malmesbury's dogs. With due allowance for hyperbole, the hundreds of thousands of Labs living throughout the world today may be likened to a huge shattered mirror, each fragment of which reflects a subtly different image of AVON.

It is important to keep that image of AVON in mind. We have seen how the launching of the Labrador Retriever breed in the United States was no less the doing of an exclusive set of wealthy patricians than had been the organized development of the breed in Britain. Yet the Lab has now evolved into the common man's buddy of choice. Is today's Lab *déclassé*? Is he essentially the luxury creature of British patricians and American plutocrats, but one that has fallen on hard times and can do a fair impersonation of the average working Joe?

It is apposite here to recall two points that confirm the Lab's credentials as a regular guy. First, the Earls of Malmesbury were the British originators of the breed and they were upstart meritocrats, not blooded patricians. Second, the Lab's Newfoundland ancestors were the furthest cry from la-di-da. They were genuine salt-of-the-sea, hardscrabble commercial fishermen's dogs squeezing a tough living out of the frigid Labrador Current.

In this chapter, we have tracked the well-documented descent of the modern Labrador Retriever from a handful of intercommunicating private kennels in nineteenth-century Britain. Yet it is equally well-documented that all of these British kennels' lines originated in, and were intermittently refreshed by, stock imported from Newfoundland. Is it possible to reconstruct with confidence the appearance and evolution of the precursors and prototypes of the Labrador Retriever in Newfoundland?

The next chapter marshals the scanty documentary evidence bearing on this perplexed question and shows that it is ambiguous, contradictory, and inconclusive. The final chapter advances a best-fit but still highly speculative scenario for the prehistory of the Labrador Retriever.

A
Newfoundland Dog's
Breakfast

T wo—and only two—modern breeds are universally acknowledged to have descended from Newfoundland ancestors exported to Great Britain before the end of the nineteenth century: our medium-sized, short-coated Labrador Retriever and our giant-sized, shaggy-coated Newfoundland. On the other hand, a score of dog-types in and from Newfoundland are to be found variously named and described in books, journals, and letters or represented in paintings, engravings, and photographs from the period of importation itself (effectively ending in the 1880s). This hodge-podge of Newfoundland dog-type terms includes (with year of first attested occurrence): *Bear dog from Newfoundland* (1732); *Newfoundland-breed* (1745); *Newfoundland Dog* (1766); *original Newfoundland Dog* (1766); *Newfoundlander* (1779); *Labrador breed of Newfoundland dogs* (1814); *St. John's breed of Newfoundland dogs* (1814); *real Newfoundland dog* (1814); *true Newfoundland dog* (1845); *Labrador Spaniel* (1847); *Lesser Labrador dog* (1847); *Newfoundland* (1847); *St John's* (1867); *Smaller Labrador* (1867); *St. John's Dog*

(1879); *St. John's Newfoundland* (1879); *genuine ancient breed of the Newfoundland dog* (1883); *Lesser Newfoundland* (1883); and, finally, *Labrador Retriever* (1894).

The correspondence between our two modern breeds and the hodge-podge of eighteenth- and nineteenth-century dog-types imputed to Newfoundland is far from unambiguous. The sources of ambiguity from the period of importation are many: the existence of distinct dog-types that may subsequently have gone extinct; the existence of a continuous range of mongrel somatypes that may have been mistakenly interpreted as several discrete breed-types; the simultaneous existence of multiple synonyms for the same dog-type; the shifting—and sometimes the complete inversion—of meaning in a given name for a dog-type over time; and, finally, inaccurate representations by writers who may have drawn on speculation, hearsay, or faulty observation.

This chapter offers a synopsis of the primary pre-1894 documentary and pictorial references to Newfoundland dogs to be gleaned both from the best modern Labrador Retriever literature and from standard reference works such as the *Dictionary of Newfoundland English* (2nd ed., 1990). Also cited are several references from the early twentieth century that bear upon the Newfoundland dog-types that were still to be observed in Newfoundland itself. Direct quotations are given where available; paraphrases are given where full quotations were unavailable; orthography and punctuation have been modernized. The synopsis is presented in chronological order through the end of the nineteenth century, with occasional historical glosses. Editorial interpretation of each historical reference in terms of antecedence to the two modern breeds is limited to a simple tentative assignment to one or the other where it seems warranted [in brackets]. Where no tentative assignment is made below, it may be inferred either that none

seems warranted or that the assignment is obvious. The various proper names that have been put forward for historical varieties of Newfoundland dogs are **emboldened** below.

The reader is invited to judge for himself whether this dog's breakfast of disjointed allusions adds up to a definite and internally consistent picture of the Labrador Retriever's prototype in Newfoundland—or just a disarticulated chimera?

1620 — Sir Richard **Whitbourne** (*A Discourse and Discovery of New-Found-Land*):

Whitbourne's mastiff dog "began to fawne and play" with "wolves" on the Newfoundland coast and disappeared with them into the woods for nine or ten days before returning unharmed. Whitbourne claimed that wolves in Newfoundland were not as "violent and devouring" as those in other countries and reported that he had been told that the natives "in the north" kept wolves, which they marked in the ears, and would avenge any wrongs done to "their wolves."

Whitbourne (died 1628) was the owner-captain of a Newfoundland fishing fleet out of the Devonshire port of Exmouth who had made his first voyage to Newfoundland in 1579. His ships having distinguished themselves in action against the Spanish Armada in 1588, Whitbourne was commissioned in 1615 to preside over the first vice-admiralty courts in Newfoundland; and in 1618 was appointed the first governor of Sir William Vaughan's Newfoundland colony on the Avalon Peninsula. The Newfoundland wolf (*Canis lupus beothucus*), extinct since about 1920, was a light-colored species closer to the northern tundra wolf than the southern timber wolf.

1732 — anon. (cited without attribution in R. Wolters: *The Labrador Retriever*, 1992)

"The **Bear dog** is of a very large size, commonly sluggish in his looks, but he is very watchful, he comes from Newfoundland, his business is to guard a Court or House, and he has a thunderous voice when strangers come near him, and does well to turn a water wheel." [*very large, shaggy, sluggish draft dog => possible antecedent of the modern Newfoundland. —ed.*]

1745 — Bampfylde-Moore **Carew** (*The Life and Adventures of Bampfylde-Moore Carew*):

"This dog was very remarkable on account of his great size, strength and unconquerable fierceness, as also for his particular aptness in the water, which is a qualification common and natural to the dogs of that country [*Newfoundland*]."

"A fine bitch of the **Newfoundland-breed** he enticed away by the art which had rendered him so famous."
[*strong, big, strong water dog => possible antecedent of the modern Newfoundland. —ed.*]
Bampfylde-Moore Carew (1693-1758).

1766 — Sir Joseph **Banks** (*The* Niger *Diary of Joseph Banks 1766*):

"Almost everybody has heard of the **Newfoundland Dogs**. I myself was desired to procure some of them and when I set out for the country firmly believed that I should meet with a sort of dogs different from any I had seen, whose particular excellence was taking the water freely. I was therefore the more surprised when told that there was no distinct breed. Those I met were mostly curs with a cross of the Mastiff in them. Some took the water well; others not at all. The thing they are valued for here is strength, as they are employed in wintertime to draw in sledges whatever is wanted from the woods. I was told indeed that at Trepassey lived a man who had a distinct breed which he called the **original Newfoundland Dogs** but I had not an opportunity of seeing any of them."

[*strong draft dog => possible antecedent of the modern Newfoundland.*
Note: first documented occurrence of the expression, "Newfoundland Dog." —ed.]

Although he was only twenty-three in 1766, Sir Joseph Banks (1743-1820) was already an accomplished naturalist who had been elected to the Royal Society. The 4th Earl of Sandwich secured Banks a berth on the H.M.S. *Niger*, which departed for a tour of duty supervising the Newfoundland fisheries in April 1766. Banks spent the summer naturalizing furiously as the ship moved from harbor to harbor around Newfoundland. On the strength of his observations in Newfoundland, Banks was chosen two years later to accompany Captain Cook in the *H.M.S. Endeavour* on his famous 1st circumnavigation. Banks went on to become the President of the Royal Society and the most renowned English naturalist of the eighteenth century.

1768 — Lt. John **Cartwright** (*Remarks on the Situation of the Red Indians…1768*):

"To complete their wretched condition, Providence has even denied them [*the Beothuk*] the pleasing services and companionship of the faithful dog."

At the direction of the Governor of Newfoundland in 1768, Lt. John Cartwright (1740-1824; in 1768, First Lieutenant on the H.M.S. *Guernsey*) led an unsuccessful inland naval expedition to establish friendly relations with Newfoundland's indigenous Indians, the Boethuk. His older brother, Capt. George Cartwright, accompanied John on his expedition and confirmed his brother's observation regarding the absence of dogs in the interior of Newfoundland in *A journal of transactions and events during a residence of nearly sixteen years on the coast of Labrador* (1792). The Boethuk, who had sought refuge in the interior wilderness from the continual massacres by English and French parties on the coast beginning in the sixteenth century, succumbed to extinction in 1829 with the death of the female captive Shanawdithit. Amongst the many ethnographic questions put to her by W.E. Cormack in 1828 was "Whether the Beothuk had any dogs amongst them or domestic animals?" Shanawdithit replied, "No." Moreover, faunal analysis of 2,900 refuse bones at the Boethuk archeological site at Boyd's Cove (AD 1100-1500) revealed no gnaw-marks diagnostic of the presence of dogs. The Boethuk were preceded on the island by Dorset Eskimos, whose archeological sites 850 BC-AD 950 have yielded to date no evidence of dogs. The Dorset culture was preceded in Newfoundland by the Maritime Archaic Indian culture. Excavations by Dr James Tuck in 1968 of a Maritime Archaic cemetery at Port au Choix on the west coast of Newfoundland yielded four complete skeletons of adult dogs, buried as grave-offerings immediately above associated human skeletons radiocarbon-dated to 1980 BC. All four dogs—the largest estimated to have weighed 45-55 lb in life—were considered to be specimens of Common Indian Dog, conforming to the description by the eighteenth-century Pennsylvanian botanist and ethnographer, John Bartram, of the dog of the northern Iroquois: "He is much more that of the wolf than of the common domesticated dogs. His body, in general, is more slender than that of our dogs. He is remarkably small behind. His ears do not hang like those of our dogs, but stand erect, and are large and sharp-pointed. He has a long, small snout, and a very sharp nose." In *Ancient People of Port au Choix: the Excavation of an Archaic Indian Cemetery in Newfoundland* (1976), Tuck concludes: "Finally, a word should be said about the relationship, or rather the lack of relationship, between these early dogs and the Newfoundland dog reputed to have been developed on the Island of Newfoundland. Our specimens possess neither the size nor the morphological structure of these large, present-day animals. The two must, therefore, be considered on present evidence to be quite unrelated."

1771-86 — Capt. George **Cartwright** (*A Journal of Transactions and Events during a Residence of Nearly Sixteen Years on the Coast of Labrador*, 3 vol., 1792):

1771 (vol. i) "He found the unfortunate Mr. Jones frozen to death, with his faithful **Newfoundland bitch** by his side. He gave the poor creature what bread he had about him, but could not prevail on her to leave her master."

1779 (vol. ii) "The bloodhound and **Newfoundlander**, which were in the shed, ran vehemently at the deer." [*Note: first documented occurrence of the expression "Newfoundlander" with reference to a dog. —ed.*]

1779 (vol. ii) "But the weather and water were so cold, that my greyhound, who has learnt from the **Newfoundland dogs** to fetch birds out of the water, would go in but once."

[*water-retriever => possible antecedent of the modern Labrador Retriever.*
Note: first documented occurrence of the expression "Newfoundland dog" in connection with fowling. Note also that this possible antecedent of the modern Labrador Retriever present in late 18th-century Labrador is called by Cartwright a "Newfoundland dog"—not a "Labrador dog." When the expression "Labrador dog" does appear almost a century later in the literature concerning Labrador, local usage applies it to the Husky (aka Eskimo Dog) [see below: Hind (1863); Grenfell (1909). —ed.]

1786 (vol. iii) "Mr Collingwood returned at three, with both the dogs; the **Newfoundlander** was lying by Alexander's gun."

In 1770, two years after he took part in his brother's inland expedition in Newfoundland, George Cartwright (1739-1819; captain in British army) undertook the operation of several fishing and sealing stations on the coast of Labrador. When his Labrador ventures failed in 1786, Cartwright returned to England and was appointed master of the army barracks in Nottingham, where he went by the sobriquet "Old Labrador."

1784 — Robert **Burns** (*The Twa Dogs. A Tale*):

'Twas in that place o' Scotland's isle,
That bears the name o' auld king Coil,
              [*Coyle*: town in Ayrshire]
Upon a bonie day in June,
When wearing thro' the afternoon,
Twa Dogs, that were na thrang at hame, [*thrang*: busy]
Forgather'd ance upon a time.
  The first I'll name, they ca'd him Ceasar,
Was keepet for his Honor's pleasure;
His hair, his size, his mouth, his lugs,   [*lugs*: ears]
Show'd he was nane o' Scotland's dogs;
But whalpet some place far abroad, [*whalpet*: whelped]
Whare sailors gang to fish for Cod." [Newfoundland]

[*exotic hair, size, mouth, ears => probable antecedent of the modern Newfoundland. —ed.*]

1795 — Aaron **Thomas** (*A Journal Written during a Journey from England to Newfoundland and from Newfoundland to England in the Years 1794 and 1795, Addressed to a Friend*):

"The celebrity of **Newfoundland Dogs** in England is so notorious that the value of them there needs no comment, but their usefulness in Britain cannot be put in competition with the great utility they are to the people of this cold country [*Newfoundland*]. In this empire of frost and snow great quantities of wood must be used by the inhabitants whose winter here is from October to April or May. The people then cut their wood for firing, for fish flakes [*drying-racks for salt cod*], and for building, etc. This wood is sometimes cut seven or ten miles in the woods and is drawn home by dogs. They have the same gearing as horses; the wood is put into sledges which they draw, and sometimes they draw a single stick only, attended by one man who wears frost shoes. This labor of dogs is daily through the winter and hard service it is. The animals here bear a more hardier aspect in general to what their same specie do in England, so much so that on superficial view their kind does not appear the same. Their difference ariseth thus—in Newfoundland the dogs commonly are their own caterers. They live chiefly on fish and many of this sturdy race fish for themselves. It is no very uncommon thing to see one of these dogs catch a fish. Bitter hunger is their monitor and as it presses upon them they go to the waterside and set on a rock, keeping as good a lookout as ever cat did for a mouse. The instant a fish appears they plunge into the water and seldom come up without their prey."

[*heavy draft and water dog => probable antecedent of the modern Newfoundland. —ed.*]

"A banker [*fisherman who fishes on the banks off southeastern Newfoundland*] is not a little proud of his dog at sea. This creature exhibited his dexterity and usefulness to a surprising degree. I shall mention the following trait as a good quality in their composition. The fishermen, when they hooked a fish, in drawing the line up the fish sometimes disentangled themselves. The fish may sometimes float in the water. The dog, observing this, dasheth into the sea and brings the fish alongside. They then throw a rope out and the dog , with the fish in his mouth, puts head into the noose of the rope and fish and dog are hauled into the vessel together. At sea those dogs often pursue and kill water fowl. I have heard of a dog who was absent from a ship on the Grand Bank for two days; on the third, he returned with a hegdown [*shearwater*] in his mouth."

[*retrieving dog light and dexterous enough to be drawn up the sides of ships in noose; possessing enough stamina to swim for two days; keen birder => probable antecedent of the modern Labrador Retriever.*

Note: first documented reference to a fishermen's retrieving water-dog in Newfoundland. —ed.]

Thomas (b.1762) was an able seaman on the *H.M.S. Boston*.

1808 — George Gordon Lord **Byron** (*Inscription on the Monument of a Newfoundland Dog*):

Near this spot
Are deposited the Remains of one
Who possessed Beauty without Vanity,
Strength without Insolence,
Courage without Ferocity,
And all the Virtues of Man without his Vices.
This praise, which would be unmeaning flattery
If inscribed over human ashes,
Is but a just tribute to the Memory of
BOATSWAIN, A DOG,
Who was born at Newfoundland, May 1803,
And died at Newstead Abbey, 18 November 1808.

[*A contemporary pencil portrait of Boatswain shows unmistakably characteristic heavy features => clear antecedent to the modern Newfoundland. —ed.*]

The monument to Boatswain still stands in the garden of Newstead Abbey, Lord Byron's ancestral home in Nottinghamshire, where he lived in intervals between 1808 and 1818 and in the chapel of which he housed his menagerie.

1809-10 — James Edward **Harris** (later **2nd Earl of Malmesbury**) (from extracts of his shooting journals 1801-1841 in *Half a Century of Sport in Hampshire*, ed. F.G. Aflalo, 1905):

December 28th, 1809, entry: "...**Newfoundland dog** that caught a woodcock in a brake at Avon cottage..." [*Note: first documented occurrence of the expression "Newfoundland Dog" in connection with field fowling. —ed.*]

November 30th, 1810, entry: "...both of which [*a snipe and a partridge*] were winged and yet, though they ran quite off, my **Newfoundland dog**, Ceasar, brought them both to us, one after the other." [*retrieving dog => possible antecedent to the modern Labrador Retriever. Note that the Newfoundland dog's name here is same as that of Burns' Newfoundland dog above. —ed.*]

1814 — Lt. Colonel Peter **Hawker** (*Instructions to Young Sportsmen in all that relates to Guns and Shooting*, 1st edition):

"NEWFOUNDLAND DOGS

"Here we are a little in the dark. Every canine brute, that is nearly as big as a jackass, and as hairy as a bear, is denominated a *fine **Newfoundland dog**.* Very different, however, is both the proper **Labrador** and **St. John's** breed of these animals; at least, many characteristic points are required, in order to distinguish them.

"The one is very large; strong in limbs; rough haired; small in head; and carries his tail very high. He is kept in that country for drawing sledges full of wood, from inland to the sea shore, where he is also very useful, by his immense strength and sagacity, among wrecks, and other disasters in boisterous weather. [*Hawker's "proper Labrador breed of the Newfoundland dog" = very large, strong, rough-haired draft and rescue dog => probable antecedent of the modern Newfoundland. Note: first documented occurrence of the word "Labrador" in connection with a dog breed. —ed.*]

"The other, by far the best for every kind of shooting, is oftener black than any other colour, and scarcely bigger than a pointer. He is made rather long in the head and nose; very fine in the legs; has short or smooth hair; does not carry his tail so much curled as the other; and is extremely quick and active in running, swimming, or fighting. [*Hawker's "St. John's breed of the Newfoundland dog" = medium-sized, black, short-haired retrieving dog => probable antecedent of the modern Labrador Retriever. Note the several glaring differences, however, from modern Lab: long in head and nose; very fine in legs; active in fighting. Note: first documented occurrence of the term "St. John's" in connection with a dog breed. —ed.*]

"**Newfoundland dogs** are so expert and savage, when fighting, that they generally contrive to seize some vital part, and often do serious injury to their antagonist. I should, therefore, mention, that the only way to get them immediately off is to put a rope, or a handker-chief, round their necks, and keep tightening it, by which means their breath will be gone, and they will be instantly choked from their hold.

"The **St. John's breed of these dogs** is chiefly used on their native coast by fishermen. Their sense of smell is scarcely to be credited. Their discrimination of scent, in following a wounded pheasant through a whole covert of game, or a pinioned wild fowl through a furze brake, or warren of rabbits, appears almost impossible...

"The **real Newfoundland dog** may be broken in to any kind of shooting; and, without additional instruction, is generally under such command, that he may be safely kept in, if required to be taken out with pointers. For finding wounded game, of every description, there is not his equal in the canine race; and he is a *sine qua non* in the general pursuit of wildfowl. [*Note that Hawker has shifted his nomenclature in this paragraph such that for "St. John's breed of the Newfoundland dog", now read "real Newfoundland dog" or simply "Newfoundland dog". That is to say, Hawker calls the probable antecedent of the modern Labrador a "Newfoundland;" and the probable antecedent of the modern Newfoundland a "Labrador"! —ed.*]

"Poole was, till of late years, the best place to buy **Newfoundland dogs**; either just imported, or broken in: but now they are become much more scarce, owing (the sailors observe) to the strictness of 'those — the tax gatherers.'"

1824 — ibid. (3rd edition, addendum under same heading):

"For a punt, or canoe, always make choice of the smallest **Newfoundland dog** that you can procure; as the smaller he is, the less water he brings in your boat after being sent out; the less cumbersome he is when afloat; and the quicker he can pursue crippled birds upon the mud. A bitch is always to be preferred to a dog in frosty weather, from being by nature, less obstructed in landing on ice.

"If, on the other hand, you want a **Newfoundland dog** only as a retriever for covert shooting; then the case becomes different; as here you require a strong animal, that will easily trot through the young wood and high grass with a large hare or pheasant in his mouth."

Lt. Col. Peter Hawker's *Instructions* became a sportsmen's bible, going through thirteen editions between 1814 and 1971. Given that the author was born in 1786 and died in 1853, he is clearly not the same Hawker of whom Lord George Scott wrote in 1933 (*op.cit.*): "between 1865 and 1875 Lord Malmesbury, Mr. C.J. Radclyffe (of Hyde, Wareham), Mr. Montagu Guest and Lord Wimborne bought a lot of black water dogs imported from Newfoundland by one Hawker, the

owner of a trading schooner, which plied between Newfoundland and Poole."

1822 — William Eppes **Cormack** (*Narrative of a Journey across the Island of Newfoundland in 1822*):

"...dogs [*of the outports on Trinity Bay*] who are admirably trained as retrievers in fowling, and are otherwise useful. The **smooth or short-haired dog** is preferred because in frosty weather the long-haired kind become encumbered with ice upon coming out of the water."

[*short-haired fowling dog => possible antecedent to the modern Labrador Retriever. —ed.*]

"A large **Newfoundland dog**, her only companion in her husband's absence, had welcomed us at the landing-place with signs of the greatest joy."

[*large size => possible antecedent to the modern Newfoundland. —ed.*]

In 1822, Cormack (1796-1868; trained in geology at Edinburgh University) and Joe Sylvester (his Micmac guide) walked across the unexplored interior of Newfoundland in an unsuccessful attempt to establish contact with the Boethuks.

1823 — Edwin **Landseer** (*Cora. A Labrador Bitch*):

This painting depicts a medium-sized bitch; dominantly black with white ticking, stockings, mouth, breast, and tail tip; long and fine in the legs; moderately feathered coat; long in the neck; broad-skulled; pendant ears set high on the skull; fairly long in the face; pointy-muzzled.

[*This bitch looks nothing like the modern Labrador Retriever. Her head and legs, however, accord with the points of Hawker's "St. John's breed of the Newfoundland dog" (1814, above).*

Note: this is the first documented occurrence of the term "Labrador" in connection with a medium-sized dog. —ed.]

Landseer (1802-1873) was the most prolific, skilled, and pricey animal painter in nineteenth-century Britain. He is best known for his many sentimental and heroic paintings of black-and-white Newfoundlands, which were consequently dubbed "Landseers" [*see Hatton & Harvey (1883), below*].

1832 — John **McGregor** (*British America*, 2 vol.):

"The **smooth short-haired dog**, so much admired in England as a **Newfoundland dog**, though a most useful and sagacious animal, and nearly as hardy and fond of water [*as the long-haired dog*], is a cross breed."

[*short-haired fowling dog => possible antecedent to the modern Labrador Retriever.*

Note: McGregor implies that although both the long-haired and short-haired water-dogs of Newfoundland are called "Newfoundland dog" in England, only the long-haired variety is in fact the true "Newfoundland dog". —ed.]

John McGregor (1797-1857).

1837 — Thomas **Bell** (*History of British Quadrupeds*):

"There are several varieties of the **Newfoundland Dog** which differ in size, character of fur, and marking. The old smooth breed, with a rather small head, white, with small black spots scattered over the body, appears now to be extinct. The largest dogs which I have met with are of the breed which I have figured. The muzzle is broad; the head is raised; the expression is noble and majestic; the hair waved or curly; the tail very thick and bushy...The color is black and white; the latter equalling, if not predominating over the former. [*author is clearly describing in preceding three sentences what will later be called a "Landseer". —ed.*] But the most common breed at present is comparatively dwarf, not exceeding in height a large water spaniel, almost wholly black, and deficient in the fine expression which may be considered characteristic of the older races." [*author is probably describing in preceding sentence an antecedent of the modern Labrador Retriever. —ed.*]

Bell was Professor of Zoology at London University; born Poole 1792.

1839 — 5th Duke of **Buccleuch** (letter, no longer extant, paraphrased in Scott-Middleton *The Labrador Dog*, 1936):

The 5th Duke of Buccleuch took his "**Labrador**" Moss and the 10th Lord Home took his "**Labrador**" Drake to Naples in the 5th Duke of Buccleuch's yacht.

[*probable antecedent of the modern Labrador Retriever.*

Note: first documented occurrence of the term "Labrador" in connection with a breeder involved in the development of the Labrador Retriever. —ed.]

According to the same source, the 5th Duke of Buccleuch's kennels were the first in Scotland to keep Newfoundland retrieving dogs, beginning as early as 1835. Other early importations by the 5th Duke of Buccleuch through Greenock were named Brandy, Drake 1840, and Nell 1848.

1840 — Delabere **Blaine** (*Encyclopaedia of Rural Sports*)

"The **St. John's breed** is preferred [*to the Labrador*] by the sportsman on every account, being smaller, more easily managed, and sagacious in the extreme. His scenting powers also are great. Some years ago these dogs could be readily procured at Poole...Indeed, gentlemen...have found them so intelligent, so faithful, and so capable of general instruction, that they have given up most sporting varieties and content themselves with these."

"The **Newfoundland dog** is easily brought to do almost anything that is required of him...and he is so tractable likewise, that with the least possible trouble he may be safely taken with pointers to the field, with whose province he will not interfere, but will be overjoyed to look up the wounded game, which he will do with a

perseverance that not speed or not distance can slacken, nor any hedgerow baulk. In cover he is very useful; some indeed shoot woodcock to a 'Newfoundland' and he never shines more than when he is returning with a woodcock, pheasant, or hare in his mouth, which he yields up, or even puts in your hand unmutilated."

[*Blaine copies Hawker (1814) in calling the probable antecedent of the modern Labrador Retriever both a "St. John's breed" and a "Newfoundland"; and the probable antecedent of the modern Newfoundland a "Labrador". —ed.*]

1842 — Joseph Beete **Jukes** (*Excursions in and about Newfoundland, during the Years 1839 and 1840, Vol. 2*):

" The day [*September 23, 1839*] before we left [*Codroy River, s.w. Newfoundland*] I bought a good dog from one of the [*Micmac*] Indians for ten shillings. Newfoundland is one of the worst places in the world for getting a good, or at least a good-looking, **Newfoundland dog**. In St. John's and its neighborhood they are the most ill-looking set of mongrels that can be conceived. In the more distant ports, however, the breed is better preserved."

"A thin, shorthaired, black dog belonging to George Harvey [*settler of Isle aux Morts, s.w. Newfoundland*] came off to us today [*September 28,1839*]. This animal was of a breed different from what we understand by the term 'Newfoundland Dog,' in England. He had a thin tapering snout, a long thin tail, and rather thin but powerful legs, with a lank body, the hair short and smooth. These are the most abundant dogs of the country, the longhaired curly dogs being comparatively rare. They are by

no means handsome, but are generally more intelligent and useful than the others. This one caught his own fish. He sat on a projecting rock...'set' attentively, and the moment one [*a Newfoundland 'sculpin' fish*] turned his broadside to him, he darted down like a fish-hawk, and seldom came up without the fish in his mouth...and when the fish did not come, I observed he once or twice put his right foot in the water and paddled it about. This foot was white; and Harvey said he did it to 'toll' or entice the fish. The whole proceeding struck me as remarkable, more especially as they said he had never been taught anything of the kind."

[*The type described here qualifies as a possible antecedent of the modern Labrador Retriever insofar as it is a shorthaired and black; but the thinness of its snout, tail, and white-stockinged legs — although according well with the analogous points in Hawker's (1814) St. John breed and Landseer's (1823) Labrador — are not characteristics of the modern Labrador Retriever. The remarkable shore-based fishing behavior accords closely with that described by Thomas (1795) above. —ed.*]

"April 2nd [*1840*]...A **Newfoundland dog** named Nestor, belonging to the Captain [*of the sealer* Topaz] jumped over into the water [*Bonavista Bay*] and swam up to it [*a young harp seal*]; but when the seal saw him approach it raised itself upright in the water and attacked him tooth and nail, biting him severely in the lip, and making master Nestor turn tail immediately. Their heads and bodies are so round and smooth, that

a dog cannot seize them anywhere except in the fippers."

Jukes (1811-1869) studied geology at Cambridge University at the same time as Charles Darwin. In 1838, at the age of 29, Jukes was appointed the first Geological Surveyor of Newfoundland on the recommendation of Professor Adam Sedgwick (also Darwin's mentor).

1842 — Richard Henry **Bonnycastle** (*Newfoundland in 1842*, 2 vol.):

"I have said nothing of the **Newfoundland dog** in the natural history section of this work...There are, however, still some splendid water dogs to be found...They are of two kinds; the short, wiry-haired **Labrador dog**, and the long, curly-haired **Newfoundland** species, generally black, with a white cross upon his breast."

Sir Richard Henry Bonnycastle (1791-1848).

1845 — William **Youatt** (*The Dog*):

"Some of the **true Newfoundland dogs** have been brought to Europe and have been used as retrievers. They are principally valuable for the fearless manner in which they will penetrate the thickest cover. They are comparatively small, but muscular, strong and generally black. [*medium-sized, black => possible antecedent of the modern Labrador Retriever. cf Hawker's (1814) "real Newfoundland dog". —ed.*] A larger variety has been bred, and is now perfectly established. He is seldom used as a sporting dog,…but is admired on account of his stature and beauty." [*large, non-sporting => probable antecedent of the modern Newfoundland. —ed.*]

William Youatt, a veterinarian and influential public health propagandist in Victorian England, described some forty varieties of domestic dog in *The Dog*.

1847 — H.D. **Richardson** (*Dogs: The Origin and Varieties*):

Richardson identifies and describes four breeds peculiar to Newfoundland:

"1. The **Newfoundland**, a dog of moderate stature, seldom exceeding twenty-six to twenty-seven inches, shaggy coated, pointed, wolfish muzzle, color usually black, with a shade of brown through it, and occasionally some white.

[*cf painting of* Cora. A Labrador Bitch *1823.*

Note: Like Hawker (1814), Richardson calls the medium-sized possible antecedent of the Labrador Retriever a "Newfoundland." —ed.]

"2. Another breed peculiar to Newfoundland is 'short-coated' and sharp nosed; is, by some, mistaken for the true Newfoundland breed…and often attains the height of 30 inches.

[*shortcoated but far too big to be antecedent to the modern Labrador Retriever. —ed.*]

"3. The **Labrador**, a much larger animal, standing 28-30 in; it had a shorter muzzle and more truncated, the upper lip more pendulous, a coat coarser, and the dog exhibiting greater strength than the Newfoundland.

[*Note: Like Hawker (1814) and Blaine (1840), Richardson calls his probable antecedent of the modern Newfoundland a "Labrador". —ed.*]

"4. The **Labrador Spaniel**, or **lesser Labrador dog**, which presents an appearance intermediate between the Newfoundland dog and the land spaniel."

[*medium-sized => possible antecedent of the modern Labrador Retriever. —ed.*]

1847 — General W.N. **Hutchinson** (*Dog Breaking*)

"From education there are a good many retrievers of many breeds, but it is generally allowed that as a rule the best retrievers are bred from a cross between the setter and the **Newfoundland,** or the strong spaniel and the **Newfoundland**. I do not mean the heavy **Labrador**, whose weight and bulk is valued as it adds to his power of draught, nor the **Newfoundland** increased in size at Halifax and St. John's to suit the taste of the English purchaser, but the far slighter dog reared by the settlers of the coast. Probably a cross from the long heavy-headed setter, who, though so wanting in pace, has an exquisite nose, and the **true Newfoundland**, makes the best retriever. Nose is the first desideratum."

[*Hutchinson follows Hawker's (1814) practice in calling the probable antecedent of the modern Labrador Retriever a "Newfoundland" or "true Newfoundland"; and the probable antecedent of the modern Newfoundland a "Labrador". —ed.*]

General Hutchinson of the Grenadier Guards wrote the standard Victorian work on dog-training.

c. 1850 — **anon.** (untitled photographic portrait of a gentleman with a dog)

This photograph shows the broad-fronted head of a medium-sized, short-coated black dog with a white muzzle. [*Based on the appearance of its head, this dog qualifies as a probable antecedent of the modern Labrador Retriever breed. Note: First extant photograph of a probable antecedent of the modern Labrador Retriever. —ed.*]

Richard Wolters acquired this untitled photograph from a New York art dealer in the 1980s and identified the sitter as the 3rd Earl of Malmesbury from his painted portraits.

1861 — Lambert **de Boileau** (*Recollections of Labrador Life*):

"The **Labrador dog**, let me remark, is a bold fellow, and, when well taught, understands, almost as well as any Christian biped, what you say to him."

[*The physical appearance of this "Labrador dog" of Labrador cannot be inferred from this excerpt. —ed.*]

1863 — Henry Youle **Hind** (*Explorations in the Interior of the Labrador Peninsula*, 2 vol.):

"The **Labrador dogs**, are excessively quarrelsome and, wolf-like, always attack the weaker."

[*wolf-like => Husky. —ed.*]

1865 — J.F. **Campbell** (*A Short American Tramp in the Fall of 1864*, Edinburgh):

"Everyone has heard of **Newfoundland dogs**, and everybody wants to get one. They ought to be pretty large, quite black, with rough waving shiny hair, black roofs to their mouths, mild wise faces, and long tails, with a slight curl at the end. The small smooth black

Labrador dog is not so much valued [as the Newfoundland dog]."

[Note: follows Bonnycastle (1842) in contrasting small, smooth-haired "Labrador dog" to the large, wavy-haired "Newfoundland"—so anticipating our modern usage. —ed.]

J.F. Campbell (1822-1885).

1866 — Henri **Herz** (*Mes Voyages en Amerique*, Paris):

On Newfoundland there are "two kinds of **Newfoundland dogs**, short-haired and long-haired. The long-haired are beyond doubt more beautiful than the short-haired, and are the only ones generally known in Europe; but the short-haired are more prized than the former in Newfoundland because they are more energetic and therefore more able to do what is asked of them; and they carry that out with eagerness and intelligence."

According to Herz, the long-haired dogs were raised for export and brought twelve to fifteen English shillings.

1867 — anon. (photographic portrait of Nell)

This photograph shows the full body of a medium-sized, broad-headed, short-coated black dog with a white muzzle and white stockings.

[probable antecedent of the modern Labrador Retriever breed. Note: Second extant photograph of a probable antecedent of the modern Labrador Retriever; similar in appearance to the dog in the c. 1850 photograph above. —ed.]

Nell was bred by the 5th Duke of Buccleuch in 1856 and owned by the 11th Earl of Home.

1867 — J.H. **Walsh** aka **Stonehenge** (*British Rural Sports*)

Stonehenge asserts that there are two types of Newfoundland: the large one that is most common in England; and the smaller one that goes by the various synonyms **St. John's**, **Smaller Labrador**, and **Newfoundland**. This smaller Newfoundland is "seldom more than twenty-five inches high and often much less."

1868 — Charles **Darwin** (*The Variation of Animals and Plants under Domestication*):

"In **dogs of the Newfoundland** , which are eminently aquatic in their habits, the skin, according to Isidore Geoffroy, extends to the third phalanges whilst in ordinary dogs it extends only to the second. In two **Newfoundland dogs** which I examined, when the toes were stretched apart and viewed on the under side, the skin extended in a nearly straight line between the outer margins of the balls of the toes."

"A nearly parallel case is offered by the **Newfoundland dog**, which was certainly brought into England

from that country, but which has since been so much modified that, as several writers have observed, it does not now closely resemble any existing native dog in Newfoundland.[87] 87. The **Newfoundland dog** is believed to be a cross between the Esquimaux dog and a large French hound. See Dr. Hodgkin, 'Brit. Assoc.,' 1844; Bechstein's 'Naturgesch. Deutschland,' Band. i. s. 574; 'Nat. Lib.,' vol. x. p. 132; also Mr. Jukes' 'Excursion in and about Newfoundland.'"

[Darwin is plainly describing here the English prototype of the modern Newfoundland. —ed.]

1869 — "Index" (pseudonymous letter published in *The Field* magazine, edited by Stonehenge):

"Around St. John's were immense numbers of close, smooth coated black dogs from 18 to 24 inches high, called **Labradors**, often admirable retrievers, which are **not true Newfoundlands** except by birth on the island."

[Note: the usage here is the exact reverse of that of Hawker (1814), Blaine (1840), and Hutchinson (1847). —ed.]

1873 — **Dinks**, **Mayhew**, and **Hutchinson** (*The Dog*):

"A retriever is a cross-breed dog. There is no true type of them. The best I have seen were a cross between the **Labrador** and Water Spaniel."

[Note: this is the same assertion as made by Hutchinson (1847), except that what the earlier writer called the "Newfoundland" is now being called the "Labrador". —ed.]

1879 — drawing by **Earle** (in J.H. Walsh *aka* Stonehenge, *The Dog, in Health and Disease*):

This drawing, captioned "**St. John's** or **Labrador Dog**", shows a heavy-set, long-headed, long-haired dog.

[This dog is far closer in appearance both to contemporary drawings of Flat-coated and Wavy-coated Retrievers and to Landseer's painting of Cora. A Labrador Bitch (1823) than it is either to the modern Labrador Retriever or to nineteenth-century photographs of Labradors belonging to Malmesbury and Buccleuch. —ed.]

1879 — J.H. **Walsh** *aka* **Stonehenge** (*The Dog, in Health and Disease*):

"In Great Britain the **small variety of the Newfoundland** is seldom kept as a mere companion, being chiefly used as a retriever…Many of these Retrievers are imported direct from Newfoundland to Hull and other ports trading with that island; others are bred in this country from imported parents…This fashionable breed, now considered a necessary adjunct to every shooter, even if he only attends a battue or drive, is often pure **St. John's** or **Labrador**; at other times he is more or less crossed with a Setter. The colour is always black without white…

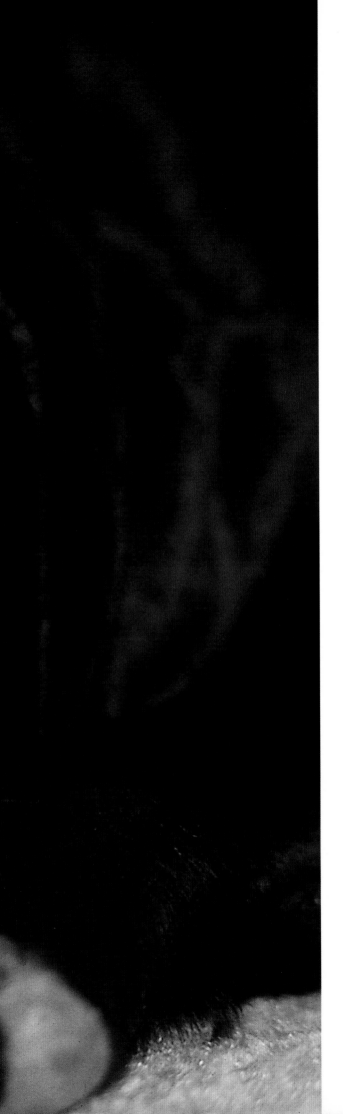

"BREED POINTS FOR THE **ST. JOHN'S NEWFOUND-LAND OR LABRADOR DOG**…

"*Neck*: Moderately long, that is to say, *as long as can be got*, imported and **pure Labradors** being often too short to stoop for a scent without difficulty…

"*Tail*: The tail is bushy without Setter feather…

"*Coat*: is moderately short, but wavy, from its length, too great for absolute smoothness. It is glossy and close, admitting wet with difficulty to the skin, owing to its oiliness, but possessing no under-coat.

"*Colour*: is a rich jet black with no rustiness. No quantity of white is admissible, but the best-bred puppies often have a white toe or star."

[*Note: These Points—constituting the first attempt, albeit informal, at a breed standard—should be read in conjunction with the above comments on Earl's drawing, with which Stonehenge illustrates his Points. The first formal Breed Standard was drawn up by the committee of the Labrador Retriever Club in 1916. —ed.*]

1881 — Capt. W.R. **Kennedy** (*Sporting Notes in Newfoundland*, St. John's):

"Packs of half-wild, half-starved curs …infest the country [*of Newfoundland*]…death to the dogs! or, at all events, to nine-tenths of them."

A few years later, the Newfoundland House of Assembly passed the Sheep Act of 1885, which permitted individual electoral districts on the island to prohibit dogs to protect the infant sheep-grazing industry. Most districts did so; others chose instead to impose prohibitively heavy taxes on bitches. The immediate and lasting effect of the legislation was that the dog population of Newfoundland was decimated.

1883 — Joseph **Hatton** & Rev. M. **Harvey** (*Newfoundland: The Oldest British Colony, Its History, Its Present Condition and Its Prospects in the Future*, London):

"Old settlers say that the **genuine** ancient breed [of the **Newfoundland dog**] consisted of a dog only about twenty-six inches high, with black ticked body, gray muzzle, and gray or white stockinged legs, with dew claws behind."

[*cf Landseer's* Cora. A Labrador Bitch (1823). *—ed.*]

"Landseer, as is well known, has immortalized one of the **Newfoundland dogs** in his celebrated picture entitled "A Distinguished Member of the Humane Society,' and the breed to which he belonged is known as the 'Landseer Newfoundland.'"

"The **Labrador**, **St John's**, or **Lesser Newfoundland**."

[*Note: Within the covers of this one book, Hatton & Harvey epitomize a century of nomenclatural confusion by variously applying the same label "Newfoundland" to three distinctly different types of dog. —ed.*]

c. 1887 — **3rd Earl of Malmesbury** (letter to 6th Duke of Buccleuch, ms.):

"We always call mine **Labrador dogs** and I have kept the breed as pure as I could from the first I had from Poole, at that time carrying on a brisk trade with New-foundland. The **real breed** may be known by their having a close coat which turns the water off like oil and, above all, a tail like an otter."

1888 — Very Rev. M.F. **Howley** (*Ecclesiastical History of Newfoundland*, Boston):

"The usual teams of shaggy and mongrel dogs were lying about and set up a terrific howl. Every house had at least seven or eight dogs, some with over 20 attached to them. One man at Port au Choix [*w. Newfoundland*] who had three teams (27 dogs) had to put up 40 barrels of herring to feed them."

[*shaggy sled-dogs => huskies—which in Labrador itself are called "Labrador dogs" {see Hind 1863, above; Grenfell 1909, below). —ed.*]

On a pastoral trip to the Labrador Straits region, Bishop Howley (1843-1914) made the above observation at Point Amour, Labrador.

1894 — **anon.** (*Pedigree of His Grace the Duke of Buccleuch's* **Labrador Retrievers** *as of August 1894*, ms.)

[*Note: the caption of this Scottish ducal manuscript contains the first occurrence of the modern expression "Labrador Retriever." —ed.*]

1906 — Norman **Duncan** (*The Adventures of Billy Topsail*, New York):

"Skipper was a **Newfoundland dog**, born of reputable parents at Back Arm [*n.w. Newfoundland*] and decently bred in Ruddy Cove. He had black hair, short, straight and wiry—the curly-haired breed has failed on the Island [*Newfoundland*]—and broad, ample shoulders, which his forebears transmitted to him from generations of hauling wood."

[*In twentieth century Newfoundland, unlike England, a short-haired water-dog might still be called indifferently a "Newfoundland dog" rather than "Labrador dog". —ed.*]

1907 — J.G. **Millais** (*Newfoundland and Its Untrodden Ways*, London):

"The best dogs are of the 'Labrador' type. In winter they are used for hauling logs—one dog will haul 2 or 3 cwt."

[*A late instance of a heavy draft-dog in Newfoundland being called a "Labrador dog" rather than "Newfoundland dog.". —ed.*]

J.G. Millais (1865-1931).

1909 — Wilfred T. **Grenfell** (*Labrador, the Country and the People*):

"The **real Labrador dog** is a very slightly modified wolf. A good specimen stands two feet six inches, or even two feet eight inches high at the shoulder, measures over six [*sic*] feet six inches from the tip of the

nose to the tip of the tail, and will scale a hundred pounds. The hair is thick and straight; on the neck it may be six inches in length. The ears are pointed and stand directly up."

"The thing that I was most afraid of down there was the **Labrador dogs**, Eskimo dogs."

[*In Labrador itself, then, "Labrador dog" was synonymous with "Eskimo dog"— the husky which in teams pulled the snow-sleds or "komatiks" full of firewood without which the permanent settlers on the Labrador coast from the 1830s until the advent of the snowmobile could not have survived the winter. —ed.*]

Wilfred T. Grenfell (1868-1940) was the humanitarian doctor who brought the first regular medical services to the Labrador Straits.

1911 — Horace G. **Hutchinson** (*A Saga of the* Sunbeam):

"One sees very few of that type which the mind associates with the name [**Newfoundland dog**], but there are many large black dogs, some with shaggy coats and some of the smoother wave, that we tend to think of as appropriate to the **Labrador retrievers**."

[*Note: Large shaggy- or wavy-coated dogs would no longer be able to be passed as "Labrador retrievers" after the Labrador Retriever Club acted in 1916 to de-legitimize any but the Malmesbury-Buccleuch smooth-coated type. —ed.*]

1913—Otto **Kelland** (*Dories and Dorymen*, St. John's, 1984):

"Half a dozen **large mongrel dogs** put in an appearance. Several of those animals were kept by men of the community [*Lamaline, on the Burin Peninsula of s.e. Newfoundland*], the dogs' main purpose in life [*being*] to retrieve salt water ducks which had been shot by their masters from dories or from the beach during the winter months. They would plunge into the icy water without hesitation as a shotgun boomed to bring down a duck, then swimming swiftly out, they would seize the dead bird in their powerful jaws returning it to the dory or beach. They were commonly called **water dogs**, a name which suited them very appropriately."

[*Note: This excerpt is a first-hand account of an event in 1913 recollected from the author's boyhood. —ed.*]

1927 — F.A. **Bruton**, ed. (in *Narrative of a Journey across the Island of Newfoundland in 1822* by W.E. Cormack, 1928):

"While I was travelling along the 'Cape Shore,' east of Placentia Bay [*s.e. Newfoundland*], in 1927, some of these smooth-haired dogs were pointed out to me as 'water-dogs'; they were said to be expert at retrieving birds that were shot, and had fallen into the water."

[*The preceding excerpt is Bruton's editorial comment on the description by Cormack (1822, above) of the "smooth or short-haired" variant of the dogs that are "admirably trained as retrievers in fowling." —ed.*]

New-Found Old Dog?

Seeking an answer to the question of the Labrador Retriever's immediate antecedents on the island of Newfoundland, we have combed the thin archives to little avail. We now turn warily to an even less promising question nested within the first: What dogs were the antecedents of the antecedents of the Labrador Retriever? On this subject, there is no primary documentation at all—the whole kit and caboodle reduces to untrammeled speculation. Without the restraint of data, no theory is too outrageous to get off the ground. The all-too-human result is that it has always been a very popular question. If the preceding chapter was a dog's breakfast, this final chapter threatens to be a mare's nest.

Some of the theories about the antecedents of the Labrador Retriever are not implausible but just unverifiable (at least not provable without the development of a much more ambitious and subtle Dog Genome Project than the one presently in progress). Such is the suggestion by Major Maurice Portal (*Guns at Home and Abroad*) that "the Fishermen of Newfoundland…crossed the heavy coated, strong black Newfoundland Retriever [*whatever that is! —ed.*] with a black Pointer" to get the St. John's breed, which is the "ancestor of the Labrador as we know him today." Such, also, is Richard Wolter's theory (*The Labrador Retriever*, 1981) that the Lab might be descended from St. Hubert's hounds that Devon fishermen might have imported to Newfoundland in the sixteenth century (despite the fact that the extinct St. Hubert's hound—ancestral to the modern Dachshund and Basset Hound—hardly looked the part and was, moreover, the exclusive preserve of the hunting nobility that would never have fallen into the possession of rude Devon fishermen; who, in any case, are never known historically to have used dogs at all in their Devon fisheries).

Other origin theories advanced for the Newfoundland dog are implausible as well as unverifiable. Such is the assertion published by Dr. Hodgkin in 1844 (as cited by Darwin in the excerpt in the preceding chapter) that "the Newfoundland dog is believed to be a cross between the Esquimaux dog and a large French hound." The implausibility here stems from the historical fact that there has been no Eskimo presence on Newfoundland since AD 950. Similarly, the theory that the Newfoundland dog was an indigenous production of the Boethuk Indians is contradicted by the documentary evidence cited above (Cartwright, 1768) that the Boethuk did not have any dogs at all.

Finally, there are the truly goofy origin theories. Such is the gormless vision of the founding couple of the Newfoundland Dog being left behind by the Vikings who planted the ephemeral settlement at L'Anse aux Meadows at the northwestern tip of Newfoundland a thousand years ago. The notion of some stalwart line of Viking dogs fiercely preserving its racial purity through five long centuries in nature dancing with wolves — followed by three more centuries in a hardly less wild human society resisting the easy virtues of European curs — is hilarious.

It is an elementary rule of population genetics that a breed can be maintained intact within a larger population of domesticated animals only under the condition of reproductive isolation. This condition can be created in either of two ways: by geographic accident or by human deliberation. In the former case, matings between animals of the same breed may be indiscriminate but the breed subpopulation as a whole is sexually insulated from animals outside the breed by geographic barriers such as water or mountains. In the latter case, human agents sequester selected breed members in special enclosures (such as kennels) and directly regulate all matings. To understand whether either of these two cases could have obtained during the early settlement of Newfoundland, we must review a little history.

The history of Newfoundland is the history of cod. The Grand Banks are uniquely fertile shoals that stretch southeast off Newfoundland for 300 miles into the Atlantic Ocean. For the whole period from shortly after their discovery by John Cabot in 1497 until shortly before their disastrous closure in 1992, the Banks reigned indisputably as the world's richest cod fishery. In *Cod: A Biography of the Fish That Changed the World* (1997), Mark Kurlansky goes it one better and asserts that the dominance of the world cod market by the Newfoundland fisheries extends back even deeper in time.

For fully half a millennium preceding Giovanni Caboto's "discovery" of Newfoundland for Henry VII of England in 1497, Kurlansky maintains, the Banks had been the secret "Hy-Brasil" fishery to which the Basque fleets each summer made the run that had enabled their continuous and mysterious domination of the European salt cod market ever since the tenth century. Assuming that Kurlansky is correct in alleging that the medieval Basque fishing fleets routinely voyaged beyond the generally known cod fisheries off Ireland and Iceland in order to fish secretly on the Banks, it is ironic to contemplate that at the same moment that Norsemen were desperately beating back Skrfllings from their little stockade at l'Anse aux Meadow on the northern tip of Newfoundland, a large Basque fleet may have been lying off the southern tip of the same island happily filling its holds with the easy cod catch.

Kurlansky argues his novel reading of history *ex silencio*. Why are the commercial records of the medieval Basque ports completely silent about fisheries off Newfoundland? To preserve their

monopolistic advantage, replies Kurlansky, the Basque fishermen conspired to keep the Banks their own deep, dark secret. But how were so many generations of Basque fishermen able to keep such a hot secret so long? Basque culture so proudly resisted assimilation to the rest of the Europe, replies Kurlansky, that secrecy amongst Basques was habitual. Even if a Basque tongue were loosened by wine, the Basque language is the unique remnant of an otherwise extinct pre-Roman language family and hence perfectly unintelligible to anybody else.

Eventually, however, even the best-kept secrets must out. Kurlansky proceeds to put a Basque spin on a long-standing and semi-respectable theory of pre-1497 European exploitation of the Newfoundland fisheries — a secrecy theory supported by a recently discovered document as well as by a mass of circumstantial evidence. It is a matter of record that, beginning in 1480, the merchants of Bristol were suddenly overcome by a collective mania to discover the magic isle of Hy-Brasil that Celtic mythology had represented since the sixth century as lying just off the west coast of Ireland; to which end, each year thenceforward, the merchants of Bristol outfitted large fleets for long westward voyages. Although these far-flung fleets were ever disappointed in their search for Hy-Brasil, they found a measure of consolation in the consistently lucky catches of cod that were reportedly taken off Ireland and Iceland.

The standard secrecy theory suggests that the Bristol merchants contrived their quest for Hy-Brasil as a blind for secret and highly profitable voyages to Newfoundland. This theory has recently been invigorated by the discovery of a letter to Christopher Columbus in which Bristol merchants accuse Columbus of having received intelligence of their discovery of North America before

he undertook his own first voyage across the Atlantic. Kurlansky seeks to preempt the Bristol-first theory by claiming that the rush of westward expeditions out of Bristol was precipitated when the Bristol merchants Jay and Croft somehow got wind in 1480 of the ancient Basque secret of the Newfoundland fisheries.

The possibility that Bristol fleets may have secretly fished the Banks before 1497 is suggested by some evidence but proven by none. The possibility that Basque fleets may have secretly fished the Banks before 1497 is suggested not by any actual evidence but rather by the paranoid supposition that a total absence of evidence must imply that blanket secrecy was imposed on a big operation. By contrast, the record of annual migratory exploitation of the Banks beginning immediately after Cabot's discovery in 1497 is abundant and varied.

The Bretons began regular transatlantic voyages to the Banks in 1504; the Portuguese before 1506; the Normans in 1506; the French Basques in 1517; the English in the 1520s; and the Spanish Basques in the 1540s. As the transatlantic migratory fisheries boomed through the sixteenth century, home ports that were advantageously placed for the national cod fleets flourished on the Atlantic coast of Europe. The entire English fleet went out the West Country ports — especially the Devonshire ports of Plymouth, Dartmouth, Bideford, and Barnstaple. Much of the Breton fleet went out of St.-Malo; the Norman out of Rouen and Granville; the French Basque out St.-Jean-de-Luz and Bayonne; the French collectively out of La Rochelle; the Spanish Basque out of the Guipuzcoan ports and the Galician ports of Ferrol and Vigo; and the Portuguese out of the ports of the Douro and Minho littoral — such as Oporto, Aveiro, and Caminha.

The cod rush rapidly matured into a huge transnational industry. From 1550 until 1750, sixty per cent of the fish eaten in Europe would be salt cod from the Banks. Already by the end of the sixteenth century, control of the cod fisheries had become so central to each of the four nations' strategic interests that only war could arbitrate the competing claims. As a result of the destruction of the Armada in 1588, the Spanish and Portuguese fishing fleets were decimated, although they were restored to a diminished level off Newfoundland during the first quarter of the seventeenth century.

After Portugal won back its independence from Spain in 1640, she formed a close diplomatic and commercial alliance with England that lasted well into the nineteenth century. Anglo-Portuguese trade remained steady and lively throughout. By preferential trade agreements, England became installed as the principal supplier of Portugal's salt fish market, in exchange for her salt, port, and citrus.

The history of the Portuguese presence in Newfoundland holds particular relevance to our story of the origin of the Labrador Retriever. In 1500, three years after John Cabot's landfall, a Portuguese navigator from the Azores, Gaspar Côrte-Real, arrived in Newfoundland; named it *Terra Nova*; claimed it for King D. Manoel I; enacted the provision of his royal charter granting him hereditary governorship; and staked the rich fishing grounds off Trinity Bay for Portugal. On a second voyage in 1501, Côrte-Real also explored the mainland coast opposite Newfoundland and christened it *Labrador* (variant spelling of *lavrador*: Portuguese for "farmworker"). Côrte-Real selected this name to advertise to potential Portuguese planters the ready supply of robust slave labor. In Labrador, Côrte-Real embarked a sample cargo of 57 strapping *labrador* candidates —probably Montagnais/Naskapi Indians — to exhibit back in Lisbon. His caravel then disappeared from history without a trace — overpowered by the cargo, perhaps?

Despite the mysterious demise of its first Governor, Newfoundland remained firmly in the Portuguese orbit. The earliest extant map showing Newfoundland is the Portuguese "Cantino" map

of 1502, on which the island of New-foundland is not labeled *Terra Nova* but rather *Terra del Rey de Portugall* ("Land of the King of Portugal"). In 1501, Cabot's royal patron, King Henry VII of England, implicitly acknowledged the parity of the Portuguese claim to the Newfoundland fisheries when he granted fishing patents to a Anglo-Portuguese consortium composed equally of Bristol and Azorean patentees.

Portuguese fishermen quickly set about opening their rich new fishing grounds off Trinity Bay, immediately adjacent to the English grounds. Beginning in 1506, King Manoel I levied a tithe on the *bacalhaos*

("codfish") arriving from *Terra Nova* through the northern Portuguese ports between the Douro and Minho Rivers. Already by 1508, a tenth of the fish sold in these same ports was Newfoundland salt cod. By 1550, Aveiro and Oporto were each sending out 150 fishing vessels to the Newfoundland fisheries.

From 1510 to 1581, Portuguese exploitation of the Banks thrived as sunny Portugal supplied overcast England cod-curing salt from its saltworks in Aveiro in exchange for English naval protection from French depredations. Throughout most of the sixteenth century, fleets of hundreds of Portuguese and English boats fished the waters off eastern Newfoundland side by side and set up their salt-curing "rooms" in adjacent bays. As the English fishing vessels were too small (on average less than 50 tons) to bring their abundant catches back to Europe, English salted cod would be loaded into capacious "sack ships" out of Portugal (displacing as much as 400 tons), which had just been emptied of the Portuguese salt that the English needed to cure their cod. This long and amicable Anglo-Portuguese cohabitation ended abruptly in 1581, as a result of the violent merger of the Portuguese and Spanish dominions under Philip II. After the naval disasters that overtook the Spanish Armada and fishing fleet in 1588, the English combined with the French to eliminate both Iberian presences off Newfoundland.

It will have been noticed that we have been at some pains to establish three points about the play of Anglo-Portuguese relations in Newfoundland: the proximity and amity of large Portuguese and English fleets in the Newfoundland fisheries in the sixteenth century; the persistence of a subordinate Portuguese presence in the Newfoundland fisheries in the seventeenth century; and the progressive strengthening of the old trade link between Newfoundland salt fish and Portuguese salt well into the nineteenth century. We confess an ulterior reason. We favor a best-fit scenario for the origin of

the antecedent of the antecedent of the Labrador Retriever that revolves around a Portuguese breed: the Cáo de Castro Laboreiro.

The Cáo de Castro Laboreiro ("Dog of Castro Laboreiro") represents our best pick for ancestor of the Labrador Retriever. The modern representative of this reputedly ancient northern Iberian peasant-livestock guardian breed looks startlingly like our modern Lab. Each of the four distinctive features laid out in the AKC Standard for the Labrador Retriever is uncannily echoed in the FCI Standard for the Castro Laboreiro Dog: broad skull fronted by moderate stop; short, close, hard coat; thick-based, dense-coated tail; and remarkable "sagacity" and performance versatility. This last feature is well exemplified by the exclusive use of Castro Labs by the armed services and aerial police of Portugal for all those specialized functions elsewhere reserved to German Shepherds.

The Portuguese breed is named after the parish of Castro Laboreiro, situated high in the Serra da Peneda in Minho, the northernmost province of Portugal. Wedged between two mountainous provinces of northwestern Spain, the Serra da Peneda is culturally continuous with Galicia. Reflecting the Gallaeci Celtic origins of the settlement, *Castro Laboreiro* means "Celtic Hilltop-Fortification for Farmworkers". So remote in its mountain fastness sits Castro Laboreiro that its Iron Age Celtic culture was largely bypassed by Romanization. Even today, the parish of Castro Laboreiro is so sparsely populated and economically unproductive that it has been incorporated into the National Park of Geres.

The mountainous and sterile terrain around Castro Laboreiro naturally favors dispersed animal husbandry over cultivation. Since time immemorial, the land has been parsed into a fixed number of modest family holdings (*minifundios*) that are preserved from partition by the practice of primogeniture. The inability of these flinty subsistence farms to support natural population

growth has traditionally encouraged the emigration of younger sons, which has never been offset by any counter current of immigration. Recalling our earlier remarks about the impossibility of preserving a domesticated animal breed without reproductive isolation, it is evident that the condition of "sexual insulation by geographic barrier" is satisfied in the case of the Castro Laboreiro Dog.

Although lowland people (and their dogs) had no reason to climb up into the indigent Serra da Peneda and breach its sexual insulation, many mountain men (and their dogs) had exigent cause to file down the Serra da Peneda to escape indigence. Denied hereditary prospects in the *minifundios*, younger sons were compelled to seek their livelihoods in the outside world. They did not have far to go. Only thirty-five miles away from Castro Laboreiro beckoned two home ports for Newfoundland cod fleets. At the mouth of the Minho River stood the Portuguese port of Caminha — one of the ports of the Minho littoral that were homes to the Portuguese cod fleets. Just across the Galician border lay the bigger port of Vigo, home to a major Spanish Basque cod fleet. The window of opportunity for the transplantation of the Castro Lab to Newfoundland is therefore three centuries wide and thirty-five miles high.

Yet two objections rise at once against the proposition that the Castro Lab might in fact have sailed through this three-century-wide window to become the Newfoundland seed of our modern Lab. The first objection says: "Even if it is granted that the modern Labrador Retriever and the modern Castro Laboreiro Dog look strikingly alike; and even if it is further granted that the parish of Castro Laboreiro was an natural museum for the conservation of biological as well as cultural forms: Still, is there any hard evidence that the Castro Laboreiro Dog actually existed as early as the sixteenth and seventeenth centuries?"

The short answer is "No." Two items of presumptive evidence may be adduced, however, in favor of the possibility that the Castro Lab was alive and well in the sixteenth century. The first item constitutes the weaker evidence. According to the Kennel Club of Portugal, the oral tradition of the parish of Castro Laboreiro holds that the dog breed is an ancient one. The second item is far more tantalizing. The full-length portrait of *Giovanni dell' Acquaviva* (Gemäldegalerie, Cassel) by Titian (*c.* 1487-1576), painted *c.* 1552, depicts standing beside its noble subject in splendid hunting array a dog that — viewed as an isolated detail — no Lab fancier would hesitate to identify as a Yellow Lab.

This seeming anachronism is seconded eighty years later in the portrait *Infante Fernando* (Prado) by Diego Velázquez (1599-1660), painted *c.* 1632-5, which again depicts beside the royal Spanish sportsman a dog about which Brian Vesey-Fitzgerald wrote in *The Domestic Dog* in 1957: "I am convinced that we have here the first portrait of the breed we know today as the Labrador. We are too apt to think of Labrador as a cold and inhospitable coastal province of Canada. It is well to remember that in Spanish it simply means a workman." Given our account above of the direct route by which the Dog of Castro Laboreiro could have found its way into maritime commerce, it would be no more surprising to find a specimen of the breed in Titian's Venice than in Velázquez' Madrid.

The second objection to the theory of a Castro Lab-Newfoundland Lab connection says: "Scorn was heaped on the Viking dog theory of the origin of the Lab because of the impossibility of preserving a breed intact without reproductive isolation. Even if it is granted that the Castro Lab could have been transplanted from Portugal to English fishing settlements in Newfoundland in the sixteenth or seventeenth century, how could a transient society of rough fishermen careless of kennels or notions of breeding have kept any breed intact for a year— much less several centuries?"

The answer is in two parts. It is readily conceded that the English fishermen on Newfoundland in the sixteenth through eighteenth centuries had no means or motive for deliberately keeping any received breed pure. Their dogs were not confined and artificially bred; they mated promiscuously. Working dogs were individual mongrels that had merited promotion from the ranks of the marginal mongrel population on the strength of accidental suitability and aptitude for the job at hand.

That the working dogs of Newfoundland were mongrels and that the marginal mongrel population was large are attested by the complaints invariably registered by those contemporary observers who actually troubled to go to Newfoundland, as evident from the citations in Chapter Three. In 1766, Sir Joseph Banks remarked: "I was therefore the more surprised when told that there was no distinct breed [of Newfoundland Dogs in Newfoundland]. Those I met were mostly curs with a cross of the Mastiff in them." In 1842, J.B. Jukes described the most abundant dog in Newfoundland in terms consistent with its being a pariah mongrel, having "a thin tapering snout, a long thin tail, and rather thin but powerful legs, with a lank body, the hair short and smooth." In 1881, Captain W.R. Kennedy inveighed against the "packs of half-wild, half-starved curs …infest the country [of Newfoundland]…death to the dogs! or, at all events, to nine-tenths of them." In 1913, Otto Kelland witnessed the savaging of some snotty French purebreeds that were visiting his natal outport on the Burin Peninsula when "half a dozen large mongrel dogs put in an appearance…[whose] main purpose in life [was] to retrieve salt water ducks which had been shot by their masters from dories or from the beach during the winter months." It is well to note that all the elaborately nuanced nineteenth-century breed classifications of Newfoundland's dogs that are cited in Chapter Three came not from observers on the ground in Newfoundland but from the pens of sportswriters who projected their subtle powers of observation from Britain's shores.

If reproductive isolation by human agency is ruled out in early Newfoundland, what about reproductive isolation by geographic barrier? Here we are on more promising ground. Just as the Castro Lab could be preserved for centuries by its reproductive isolation in the mountains of Portugal, so it could have been preserved for centuries by reproductive isolation in certain remote Newfoundland fishing communities.

The history of Newfoundland — it bears repeating — is the history of its cod fisheries. From the beginning of the sixteenth through the middle of the eighteenth centuries, the annual commercial cycle never altered. Every April, fleets manned by scores of thousands of fishermen would race on the prevailing easterlies 2,200 miles across the Atlantic to Newfoundland in order to claim the best fishing "rooms" (beaches suitable for the sprawling business of drying and curing the catch). The cod on the Grand Banks migrate in close to the Newfoundland shore to spawn in warmer waters in July and August. Inshore fishing from shore-launched dories was therefore the dominant activity in these months. In September, the cod swim as much as three hundred miles back out to the Banks to bottom-feed in nutrient-rich colder water for another year. Fishing therefore continued on the Banks from late summer through the fall, mainly in dories dropped from deep-hulled ocean-going ships. For both inshore fishing and banking, the same dories were used: twenty-foot skiffs crewed by two or three fishermen — except in the case of the notoriously abused Portuguese fishermen, who were sent out solo.

The skiffs were deckless and low-gunwaled to expedite the hauling in of the cod one-by-one on baited hand-lines. Once their three-foot-deep holds were filled to capacity by some 300 cod, the

dories became unseaworthy and prone to foundering. Dory catches were loaded into the mother ships, brought ashore to the fishing rooms, processed, and loaded into sack ships. At the end of the fishing season in November, the mother ships too were loaded and Newfoundland's whole floating population sailed back to Europe on the prevailing westerlies.

The place of the fisherman's dog was in the dory. A cod's muscles are twitchy but weak, as befits a suspended bottom-feeder. A cod being hauled up through 15-30 fathoms quickly weakens and spends its fight. Consequently, when a cod flipped off the hook or over the side it would float dazed on the water for a short time. The duty of the dog was to retrieve on command before the cod revived and swam off. The dog must be nimble, biddable, and hard. Spillage during the trans-

fer of the dory's catch to the mother ship was the other occasion that called upon the water dog's retrieving skills.

Official English attempts to plant settlements on Newfoundland in 1583 and 1623 failed. The wealthy fleet-masters (known as the *Western Adventurers*) opposed any colonization of Newfoundland as a threat to their monopolistic control of fishing grounds, fishing rooms, and trade privileges. They successfully lobbied for legislation enacted in 1634 prohibiting settlement within six miles of shore, forbidding fishermen to remain behind after the close of fishing season, and requiring a special license to build or repair any house. In 1654, the licensed population of Newfoundland numbered only 1,750 people, concentrated in fifteen small settlements, most on the eastern shore. Yet an unlicensed shadow population of at least

equal size lived in tiny illegal settlements hidden in remote coves on the Newfoundland coastline.

This shadow population was composed of deserters and descendants of deserters going back to shadowy times. Deserters ran from the fishing vessel captains, from the shore merchants, and from the British Navy (which had charge of regulating the fisheries and enforcing the settlement prohibitions). It is important to understand two peculiarities of British life at sea in the sixteenth through eighteenth centuries. First, all three maritime branches are known to have embarked women in various capacities on voyages. Secondly, desertion was not an exceptional reaction to abuses in the Navy, but a steady-state feature of all maritime branches. Well into the nineteenth century, one fifth of merchant seamen sailing from St. John's deserted in the course of each voyage.

It is not strange that crewmen (designated "servants") should have run from civilian vessels and shore employment at least as often as from men-o'-war. Discipline was no less brutal in fishing vessels and rooms than on naval vessels; cheating out of wages was more rampant; and the justice meted out by the plenipotent captain of a fishing vessel to his crew was liable to be even more arbitrary than that which was in the Navy nominally restrained by Admiralty Regulations.

But as many as were the provocations to desertion, the opportunities to make a clean jump in Newfoundland were more numerous still. Moreover, even when the servant stuck it out to season's end, he all too often found himself cruelly abandoned on the wintry shores of Newfoundland in order to save the master the cost of his passage home — in spite of laws mandating the return of all crew. Thousands of deserters and desertees smuggled themselves on opportunistic Yankee traders down to New England. Thousands of others searched out remote niches to occupy in Newfoundland.

Thanks to eustatic flooding, the coastline of Newfoundland is one of the most indented in the world. Superimposed in the island's basic triangular outline is a nervous jiggle of deep fjords, inlets, coves, and bays that offered safe haven to both pirates and deserters. Communities of deserters naturally sited themselves where they might best avoid detection by fellow-Englishmen; yet where the fishing was good; and, lastly, where they might best conduct occasional trade with foreign fishermen, who were the only safe contact with the outside world from whom to procure such external necessities as salt and ammunition.

Not until the middle of the eighteenth century was the power of the merchant-adventurers broken; or martial rule by the Navy relaxed to accommodate a measure of colonial self-rule; or the 1634 and 1699 legal impediments to settlement rescinded. By the time the cove communities could finally dare to emerge into the light, they were fossils of another age. Even after they became lawful, these cove communities retained their cultural and physical insularity. Newfoundland's first road (nine miles from St. John's to Portugal Cove) was not built on until 1825. Well into the twentieth century, many of these cove communities remained inaccessible except by harrowing voyages in small vessels. And to this day, many a cove community speaks its own queer dialect, quite distinct from any other. Historical linguists have identified various of these Newfoundland cove community's dialects as perfect sixteenth-century relics of precise localities in the West Country of England, whence the community's founders were recruited.

Where dialect can be preserved uncontaminated from a point in time four centuries ago, so can a dog breed. Denied any future contact with the outside dog world, all issue from original purebred ancestors must be like-to-like and therefore purebred, too. And how might such original

purebred Castro Laboreiro Dogs have been introduced into a cove community? Sited in accordance with the deserters' preference for a coastline unfrequented by Englishmen yet offering occasional commercial contact with foreign fishermen, the English cove communities off the sixteenth-century Portuguese fishing grounds north of the Avalon Peninsula seem excellent candidates both as the ports-of-entry and the open-air purebreed kennels for the Castro Laboreiro Dog in Newfoundland.

One can credit without undue strain a scenario whereby at the end of a fishing season a Portuguese fishermen with a sack of salt to barter for a quintal of cured English cod might not be adverse to trading his hungry dog as well just before the long idle voyage back to Minho, where he could easily get another. A Castro Lab line, once launched in a cove community, would remain pure in the absence of outside dogs but would be subject to selective pressures for performance traits by the human owners. Castro Labs who failed to perform usefully as retrievers in fishing and fowling would be highly liable to culling in a microsociety never far from the brink of starvation. The process of continual culling for performance aptitudes could explain the incremental behavioral transformation of the Castro Lab from a mountain livestock guardian into a water retriever whilst retaining its physical attributes.

Is there any evidence for this devious line of speculation? Actually, there is. First, the very name of the Labrador Dog — a native of the island of Newfoundland that never had any demonstrable thing to do the bleak and frigid Labrador mainland, which had no permanent

settlers until the 1830s and where the only dogs of use to the beleaguered settlers were the komatik teams of mongrel huskies — proclaims its Portuguese connection. *Labrador* (the Newfoundland dog) is a natural English corruption of the word *Laboreiro*—refracted into its more familiar Portuguese cognate, *Labrador* (the mainland coast). The latter toponym supplies the attributive sense of *Labrador* in the homophonic expression *Labrador dog* that refers to the husky of Labrador.

Secondly, the vital connection between the indigenous Labrador and the cove communities is a proven fact. The most melancholy of the many mysteries investing the history of the Labrador Retriever concerns the fate of the indigenous Labrador breed of Newfoundland in the twentieth century. From being a much-remarked (though scarce) export item to Britain in the nineteenth century, the indigenous Labrador breed slipped into total eclipse in the twentieth century. No Labrador Retriever has ever been registered in Newfoundland that was not wholly descended from British stock. Only twice in the twentieth century have exhaustive searches of the Island of Newfoundland succeeded in turning up any indigenous dog specimens that look like the original Malmesbury and Buccleuch Labradors of the photographs. Both discoveries were made about thirty years ago — in remote cove communities!

Here is the key to the oft-asked question, "Why did the indigenous Labrador breed suddenly plunge to extinction level in the twentieth century?" Most Lab writers appeal to late nineteenth-century anti-dog legislation or to improvements in fishing technology that marginalized the utility of a water dog. But the considerations of population genetics taken up in this chapter point to another explanation. These considerations argue that the Newfoundland breed of Labradors that fed the Malmesbury-Buccleuch lines in Britain was never very abundant in Newfoundland itself because it could not be preserved there except in hermetically remote cove communities. Purebred cove Labs that were sold to work out of local ports such as St. John's would breed promiscuously and melt into the cosmopolitan mongrel population. Conversely, outside mongrels (or French purebreeds, for that matter) that exploited a new route into an untouched cove community would quickly adulterate its pure Lab stock.

The ending of the indigenous Labrador breed in Newfoundland was a direct consequence of the ending of four hundred years of solitude in the most remote cove communities. It is no coincidence that the few pure Castro Laboreiro Dogs to be found today in the parish of Castro Laboreiro are — like the Labrador Retrievers to be found today in Newfoundland — all derived from outside commercial kennel-stock. The indigenous Castro Lab has suffered the same mournful fate as its cousin in Newfoundland — and for the same reason.

Just as radio, television, and state education have contaminated the fossilized Elizabethan dialects of even the loneliest cove communities in Newfoundland; so did the intrusion of motorized boats, roads, and railroads breach the reproductive isolation of the last living Castro Lab fossils in the farthest outports and so deliver the genetic death-stroke to the indigenous Labrador breed. Only timely foreign intervention by a consortium of private patrician breeders in the last century saved from unnoticed extinction the outlaw breed of Newfoundland that has gone on to conquer the respectable dog world. Hail the new-found old dog!